msel Daly, D.V.M
ron Vanderlip, D.V.M.

Rats

Everything About Purchase, Care,
Nutrition, Handling, and Behavior

BARRON'S

CONTENTS

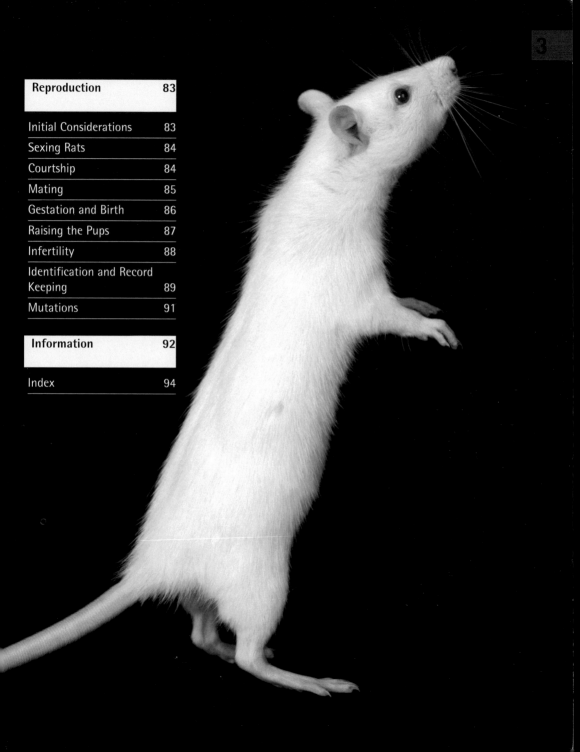

3

INTRODUCTION TO RATS

The group of animals that zoologists call rodents comprises almost 40 percent of all mammals. By sheer numbers, these animals have been tremendously successful. But their success can also be measured by their diversity of form and ability to adapt to nearly every type of climate on earth.

You may be quite surprised to learn just what your rat's relations are! Rats are rodents, and rodents rank among the most diverse and numerous of mammalian species. Rodents are remarkably uniform in structural characteristics. They are divided into three groups based on similarities in anatomical characteristics, teeth and bone structure, skull and skull muscles, origin, and lifestyle.

Rodents are classified into related groups called families. There are 29 rodent families in existence today. The rat belongs to the Muridae family, which is the largest mammalian family, containing 267 genera (genus) and about 1140 species (with new species being continually discovered!). Included in the Muridae family are rats, mice, and hamsters.

A second group of rodents includes nearly 380 species, including squirrels, marmots, beavers, gophers, and woodchucks. The oldest

known rodent fossil from this group is recorded to be approximately 60 million years old.

Guinea pigs, chinchillas, porcupines, and the biggest rodent, the capybara, all belong to the third group of animals called cavy-like rodents, of which there are about 190 species.

Common to these seemingly diverse groups of rodents is a characteristic bony jaw structure and associated muscles that give these animals the ability to gnaw through nearly everything. In fact, the word "rodent" is derived from the Latin *rodere,* which means "to gnaw." Rodents have four opposing incisors, two in the upper jaw and two in the lower. These teeth grow continuously throughout the animal's life, a phenomenal 5 inches (12.5 cm) each year. Between the incisor teeth and the grinding molars is a space called the diastema. The absence of canine teeth and premolars allows a rodent to draw its lips into its mouth

Physical Characteristics of Wild Rats

	Rattus norvegicus	Rattus rattus
Weight	10–17 oz. (280–480 gm)	4–12 oz. (113–340 gm)
Length	12–18 in. (32–46 cm)	14–18 in. (35–46 cm)
Body Shape	chubby	slender
Muzzle	short	elongated
Ears	less than ¾ in. (2 cm), covered by fine hairs	more than ¾ in. (2 cm), hairless
Tail	shorter than length of body and head combined	longer than length of body and head combined

Zoologists use skull type, size, musculature, and other physical characteristics to classify rats into different species. The table above lists differences between the two most common species of wild rats—R. norvegicus and R. rattus.

behind the incisors. This effectively closes off the rest of the oral space as the animal gnaws.

Rodents are resourceful consumers, capable of handling a wide variety of foods. All rodents are omnivorous, adapting their diet to whatever food is available. Some species have adapted to environments with little water. The most successful of all rodents, rats and mice live close enough to humans to partake of their bounty and find shelter in their dwellings. Other species have evolved physiologic mechanisms that allow them to live in climates with extreme temperatures.

The Nature of Rats

The mouse-like rodents, which include rats, probably originated in the Southeast Asian islands, India, central Asia, and China before the Ice Age. When the shipping trade with this part of the world began, so did the worldwide distribution of rats. First to invade Europe was the black, or roof rat, *Rattus rattus*. This occurred around the twelfth century, and by the sixteenth century, the black rat had arrived in America. The larger and more aggressive brown rat, *Rattus norvegicus*, invaded Europe several hundred years later, in the early eighteenth century, but spread rapidly. Within 100 years, brown rats were established in America as well. There are many other species of rats,

Rat Taxonomy
Kingdom *Animalia*
Phylum *Chordata*
Class *Mammalia*
Order *Rodentia*
Suborder *Myomorpha*
Family *Muridae*
Genus *Rattus* (more than 137 species!)
species *norvegicus*

possibly several hundred, distributed around the world. In the United States and in most other countries, the two most important species of rats to share man's habitat remain *Rattus norvegicus* and *Rattus rattus*.

R. norvegicus and *R. rattus* can be distinguished by physical characteristics, by the way they behave, where they are likely to be found geographically, and by habitat. Rat-control officials and public health agents make use of these differences in eradication programs necessary to control populations of wild rats in urban and rural areas.

R. norvegicus, the species from which all domestic pet rats are derived, is the larger of the two species. It weighs between 10 and 17 ounces (280–480 gm) and ranges in length from 12 to a remarkable 18 inches (32–46 cm). Its body is round and tapers toward the neck. Its nose or muzzle is relatively short and its ears are small, usually less than ³/₄ inch (2 cm) in length, and are covered with fine hairs. Its tail is usually shorter than the length of its head and body.

The roof rat, *R. rattus,* can also grow to a length of 14 to 18 inches (35–46 cm). However,

Rat Facts

Scientific name	*Rattus norvegicus*
Common names	Norwegian rat, common brown rat, gray rat, wharf rat
Origin	Central Asia or China
Coat Color, Length, Texture	Various coat colors, patterns, length, textures
Behavior	Territorial, social, colonial
Lifestyle	Opportunistic and adaptable, living in colonies in areas close to human habitation
Life span	2½ to 3½ years

this rat is more slender and weighs between 4 and 12 ounces (113–340 gm). Its nose is more elongated. Its ears are not covered with fine hairs and are generally longer than ³/₄ inch (2 cm). The tail may be longer than the head and body combined.

Behavior in Wild Rats

The brown rat may seem lumbering at potentially twice the body weight of the roof rat, but don't be fooled! Despite their size, they can enter buildings and other spaces through very small openings. They can leap distances of eight feet from a standstill and heights of two to three feet.

Roof rats are better acrobats than their cousins, although brown rats are fiercer and will drive roof rats away. If they do share buildings, roof rats are likely to be found above the ground floor, with brown rats closer to the basement and foundation. To reach such heights, a rat takes advantage of any surface on which it can get a toehold, even scaling a vertical wall. If the wall is smooth, a rat braces its back against a parallel drainpipe. Inside walls, they travel between nails and

Rat Dental Formula

2 (I 1/1, C 0/0, P 0/0, M 3/3) =16
I = Incisors   C = Canine teeth
P = Premolars   M = Molars

The number above the slash represents half of the upper jaw, and the number under the slash represents half of the bottom jaw.

In the rat, there are no canine teeth or premolars.

There is one incisor in the upper jaw right side and three molars in the right side of the upper. There is one opposing incisor on the bottom jaw right side and three opposing molars in the bottom jaw right side. These total eight teeth. Multiply eight by two, to include all the teeth on the left side of the mouth, and the total number of teeth equals sixteen.

stud boards less than 18 inches (46 cm) apart. Rats also use clotheslines and telephone lines as circus high wires to get from one place to another.

During warm months, brown rats leave the protection of buildings and migrate into the

Rat Biology

Natural habitat in the wild	Areas near human habitation, cities, wharfs, alleys, farms
Number of chromosomes (diploid)	42 (21 chromosome pairs)
Body temperature	99.5 to 100.5°F (35.9 to 37.5°C)
Heart rate	330 to 480 beats per minute
Respiratory rate	70 to 114 breaths per minute
Food consumption	.35 ounces (10 g) of food per 3.5 ounces (100 g) of body weight per day
Water consumption	2.7 to 3.7 ounces (80 to 110 ml) per 3.5 ounces (100 g) of body weight per day

countryside to find plentiful food supplies on farms. In rural places, these creatures live in elaborate labyrinths of burrows with multiple entrances and exits. These habitats are usually no deeper than 18 inches (46 cm) underground. Sometimes roof rats take over burrows abandoned by brown rats.

Rats as Pests

As a rat fancier, you are a member of a growing number of people who recognize these animals as delightful companions. However, after many centuries, rats earned the reputation of being highly destructive and carriers of disease. They destroy dwellings, crops, and stored food. They spread disease through their urine and feces, through bite wounds, and by acting as hosts to disease-carrying fleas.

Wild rat populations depend on two factors: food supply and harborage. Predictably, rats are prevalent in areas that have poor sanitation, careless disposal of garbage, and easy access to stored food. Unless a building is specifically "rat-proofed," they will enter it looking for food and shelter.

A Positive Note

It should be emphasized, lest you are left looking in horror at your pet rat, that the foregoing description of the relationship between rats and humans pertains to populations of wild rats, not the domesticated variety. With selective breeding, careful husbandry, and medical care, domestic rats have become less aggressive, more accustomed to confinement, and free from dangerous diseases carried by their wild counterparts.

Rats have powerful jaw muscles that enable them to chew through lead, uncured concrete, and adobe brick. Aside from the direct destruction, rats contaminate food with their urine, droppings, hair, and dander, making the food unfit for consumption.

Rats and Diseases Contagious to Humans

Historically, rats have been responsible for the deaths of millions of people. During the fourteenth century, three major epidemics of plague swept across Europe. Bubonic plague, caused by the bacterium *Yersinia pestis,* is fatal to rats, too. People died in massive numbers when they came in contact with rat carcasses or were bitten by rat fleas carrying the bacteria. Remember that sanitation, as we know it, was almost nonexistent at the time. Rats flourished in the garbage and sewage thrown into the streets. Around the world, cases of bubonic plague continue to occur, even in modern, industrialized societies.

There are other bacteria and viruses that can be transmitted from wild rats to humans, such as the bacterial disease leptospirosis. *Leptospira* germs are harbored by wild rodents and transmitted primarily to livestock through drinking water contaminated with rat urine. In farm animals, dogs, and humans, leptospirosis results in liver, kidney, and reproductive diseases.

Special Senses

Of the five basic senses, the sense of *sight* is the least developed in rats. Although they are unable to see in great detail, rats do distinguish strongly contrasting shadows of light and dark. Rats do not see colors. They are good at judging distances and are accurate jumpers. To compensate for poor vision, the sense of *touch* is very well developed in rats. Free-roaming rats prefer to move along walls by using the vibrissae, or whiskers, on either side of the face. In addition, there are longer tactile hairs scattered over the body that help the rat to maneuver through burrows and other confined spaces.

Rats can *taste* about as well as humans, and they also have a strong attraction to sweets! Their sense of *smell*, however, is very keen and plays an enormously important role in reproduction and breeding. Rats can *hear* well, too. They respond more strongly to loud, sharp noises than to low, repetitive ones.

Communication

Rats communicate primarily through vocalizations (sounds), scent, touch (grooming, huddling), and visual cues (body language).

Sound: Rats have a very keen sense of hearing. Rats are normally quiet animals, but they are capable of making a variety of sounds (vocalizations), especially if they are fright-

Rat Body Language

Behavior	Meaning
Running, hopping, twisting ("frisky hops"), wrestling, rolling on back	Play behavior
Submission	Head lowered, ears laid back against head; if cornered or frightened, may take on a defensive posture and lay on back with fore limbs raised
Dominance	Raises head above the subordinate rat and may lay its head on top of the other rat
Fur raised all over body (pilo-erection)	Aggression, fear
Tail raised or held out stiffly	Aggression, fear, in retreat
Standing on hind limbs facing each other for prolonged period of time	Aggression
Fighting with forepaws	Rebuke, aggression

Rat Communication

Sound	Meaning
Squeak	Irritated, angry, frightened, defensive
Squeal	Pain, fear, fighting
Tooth grinding	Depending on the circumstances, may be pain or may indicate being happy and at ease
Teeth chattering	Stress, may indicate respiratory distress
Ultrasonic sounds (outside of human hearing range)	Baby rats' call to mother

and feces), and when they are receptive to breeding.

Tactile: Through sense of touch, rats demonstrate compatibility, as in grooming one another and huddling together to sleep.

Sight (vision): Rats do not have sharp vision; however, they use their vision to interpret their body language. Rats can see in subdued lighting, and, with the tactile information they receive from their whiskers, they are able to navigate well in the darkness.

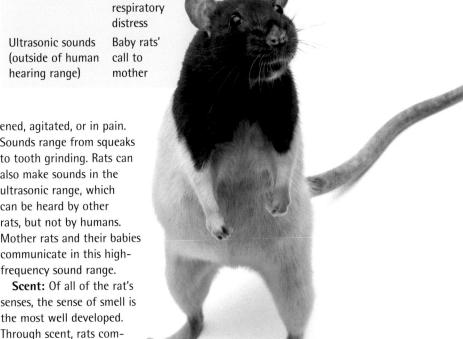

ened, agitated, or in pain. Sounds range from squeaks to tooth grinding. Rats can also make sounds in the ultrasonic range, which can be heard by other rats, but not by humans. Mother rats and their babies communicate in this high-frequency sound range.

Scent: Of all of the rat's senses, the sense of smell is the most well developed. Through scent, rats communicate information, such as marking their territory (with urine

OBTAINING A RAT

*Domesticated rats,
labratory rats used
in research and those
we keep as pets,
originated from the
wild rat species
Rattus norvegicus.*

What Kind of Rat Is This?

In the 1800s, it was common for people in Europe to keep rats for sport. Hundreds of brown rats were trapped and used for rat baiting, a form of gaming where rats were placed in a pit with a ferocious terrier. Bets were placed on the dogs and the time it would take to kill every last rat. Rats with unusual coat colors, particularly albinos, were spared and used for breeding and shows.

Around 1890 rats began to be used in scientific research in the United States. The origin of these rats is not clear. Some were brought by scientists from Europe coming to study in Philadelphia at the newly established Wistar Institute; others were probably wild-caught from the streets of the city itself. Prized for their prolific nature, rapid growth, small size, and willingness to accept human contact, rats were sent to universities all over the country. With their endearing personalities, it's no wonder that rats also made their way into homes as pets.

Varieties of Rats

Body size and shapes of dogs and cats vary with each breed (e.g., Golden Retriever, German Shepherd, Maine Coon, or Siamese) within the species, but there are no true breeds of rats. However, there are four main "varieties" of rats:

1. standard
2. dumbo
3. hairless
4. tail-less

The standard wild *Rattus norvegicus* has an agouti or ticked coat with a white or cream-colored underbelly. Agouti hairs are banded. Close inspection of each hair shaft reveals that it is striped by three colors: grayish blue next to the skin, yellow in the middle, and black on the tip. This banding pattern provides an excellent camouflage; nature has used it in many animal species, from Agoutis to Abyssinian cats, to jackrabbits.

Fancy rats—those varieties that have been bred for show and pets—do not all have an agouti coat. There are many variations in coat color, marking pattern, and texture. The variety in appearance of rats is determined by modification of the rat's chromosomes. Chromosomes are packages of information inside every cell that determine such traits as how long the tail will grow, what color the eyes will be, and whether the hair will be curly or straight. Each one of these traits is carried on a specific place on the chromosome called a gene. Over time, the information carried in genes can change, or mutate. When this happens, offspring that look different from the parents emerge.

Pet rats can now be found in a wide variety of coat colors, patterns, and coat textures, as well as three basic body conformation types. Definitions of colors vary according to clubs and their standards and guidelines, but as many

Selective Breeding

Serious rat breeders keep careful records and study the colors and markings of offspring produced through planned mating of parents with known genetics. They can predict with some certainty what the offspring will be like. Many beautiful colors and patterns have been produced through selective breeding.

as 30 colors and shades are recognized. These include the basic "wild type" coloration known as agouti, as well as black, beige, blue, and white. Color patterns include solid, or "self-colored" rats, or hooded rats. Hooded rats have a colored head or "hood" with coloration that extends over the shoulders and partway down the back.

Solid rats are found in a variety of colors: dark brown, black, chocolate, gray, lavender (very light gray, almost blue), lilac, yellow, sand, and silver. Albino rats, also called pink-eyed whites (PEWs), have no pigment at all.

There are six coat types:

1. Standard smooth coat: this is the most common coat type. It is the type that we usually think of when we consider rats, and it is the coat type most often found on rats in pet stores.

2. Satin: Satin coats have a glossy sheen to them and the coat hairs are fine. Satins occur in all coat colors and patterns. Wavy, curly, or bent whiskers are common.

3. Rex: Rex coats are dense and evenly curled. All coat colors and coat patterns are acceptable. Whiskers are curly.

4. Velour: Velour coats are soft, fuzzy, and short.

5. Velvet: Velvet coats are very sleek and soft to the touch. They are short and plush.

6. Hairless: Hairless rats have thin, healthy, essentially hairless skin. Hair is very short and fine, almost imperceptible. In the hairless category are also the patchwork hairless. The short, fine hairs on the body grow in patterns such that there are areas, or patches, or hair loss in some parts of the body while there are areas of fine hair growth in other parts. The hair growth patterns vary, so that the animal's appearance changes over time. The amount of skin pigmentation may vary. Ears are large and wrinkle free. Whiskers may be straight or curly, present or absent.

For show purposes, rats are divided into categories, and these categories may vary according to individual rat clubs and guidelines. Many clubs recognize these six main categories for rat competitions:

1. Standard: Short, smooth coat (various coat colors and patterns) that covers head and body, small ears.

2. Dumbo: Ears large, round, and set low on the sides of the head (various coat colors and patterns).

3. Hairless

4. Satin

5. Rex

6. Tail-less: The tail-less rat is characterized by a complete absence of tail and a body that is more round and compact than the typical rat. All colors are acceptable for tail-less rats. As a point of information, tail-less rats are not commonly found, and rat breeders report that they encounter more health problems and malformations among animals in their colonies when they are breeding and raising tail-less rats. This raises the question of whether the gene(s) responsible for a rat not having a tail might not also be linked to other genetic problems in some cases. Although some people might prefer a rat that doesn't have a tail, the fact is that rats use and need their long tails for balancing and for body language communication.

Behavior of pet rats can also be linked to color and coat pattern. For example, white rats have very calm temperaments. Hooded rats are

generally more active, may be more aggressive, and are therefore, more challenging to handle and restrain.

Show Rats

Showing rats in competition isn't new; people have been showing rats for more than 100 years. It has grown in popularity as rat clubs have been created and organized and standards in conformation have been adopted. In rat shows, animals of each variety compete against each other. They are judged based on conformation, or how closely they fit the physical characteristics defined by the club standard, coat color, and texture. The animal must also appear healthy and friendly.

Rat shows take place regionally around the United States. The judges are people who are involved extensively in the fancy: They usually breed and raise rats, and promote rats through their club activities and Internet connections.

Rat standards: There is increasing movement in the rat fancy toward uniformity in the definition of what constitutes the "ideal" rat conformation between the rat clubs across the country and around the world. There are also efforts toward standardization in defining coat colors and markings.

Rat Registries

A number of the larger national and international rat clubs and even smaller local clubs are encouraging their members to register their rats and their offspring.

Rat registration is a topic of some contention within the rat fancy community. Most clubs and shows don't require that you register your rats in order to belong to the club or to breed, show, or sell them. If you are serious about becoming involved in rat fancy outside of caring for a few as pets, you should check with your club for the rules governing participation in these activities.

Considerations Before You Choose Your Rat

Why adopt a rat?

Rats are small and quiet. They do not take up much space in the home, are inexpensive to feed, and easy to clean. You never have to take them out for a walk in the rain. Rats don't howl during thunderstorms. Rats don't need vaccinations or a county license. You can take them with you on vacation or ask a friend to look after them. Many landlords accept "small animals in cages" as tenants.

Rats are good companions for people who don't have much time to devote to their care, socialization, and training although they live happier and healthier when socially enriched. The elderly and shut-ins may enjoy looking after one or two rats because of their small size and the relative ease of cleaning the habitat. Classroom rats are an excellent learning tool. Children learn about nature, intelligence, and nutrition, as well as about the responsibility of caring for animals.

T I P

Registry Facts

It's very important for anyone thinking about registering their animals, or anyone purchasing registered animals, to remember that *registration is not a guarantee of quality*. It is merely a listing of parents and offspring.

The goal of most rat registries is not to promote exclusivity or define or guarantee quality, but to serve as a central record. By maintaining the registry and studying the animals for disease incidence, tumor development, behavior characteristics, longevity, and so on, it may be possible to minimize the occurrence of health problems through selective breeding. Rat registries also serve as a database to define coat colors and markings.

Rats are interesting, intelligent pets. They are easy to please and they recognize and trust their owners. They can even learn to do many tricks. Pet owners feel needed because their pets depend on them for food and care. Best of all, rats are very good at providing companionship and entertainment for the people who care for them.

It is well documented that people benefit greatly from pet ownership. People derive physiological and psychological benefits from the human–animal bond they form. For example, caressing or holding a pet has been shown to reduce blood pressure in some people. It has even been shown to increase oxytocin release

TIP

Questions to Ask

Here are some questions that anyone who is thinking of adopting or buying a rat (or any pet) should answer and discuss with everyone at home who might come in contact with or be affected by the animal. When they are answered to your satisfaction, you can get down to the business of finding your rat.

✔ Do you have the time each day to feed, water, and clean your rat's habitat?

✔ Do you have the time each day to exercise and play with a rat?

✔ Do you have a readily available source of a balanced rodent diet?

✔ Do you have enough money to buy or build a safe habitat of adequate size? Do you have a place to put this habitat?

✔ Are all household members able to understand how to hold and play with a rat? Are some of the children too young or play too rough to do this?

✔ Is anyone in your household allergic to animals?

✔ Will the other pets at home accept a new arrival?

✔ What happens if your rat gets sick? Will you be willing to take it to the veterinarian?

✔ Do you know a veterinarian who can take care of sick rats? Do you know how much it might cost for your rat to be examined? Do you understand that it may cost just as much to have your rat examined and treated as it would a more conventional pet such as a dog or a cat? The cost of veterinary care is not predicated on the purchase price of the pet.

✔ Who will care for your rat when you go on a trip?

✔ Did you know that rats are destructive when left to their own devices and leave droppings and urine on you and around the house? Are you prepared to "rat-proof" your house?

in some pet owners. Oxytocin is a hormone that plays an important role in bonding, trust, desire for social connection, and stress reduction. So if you think you are happier and feel better after holding your rat, you probably do!

It is truly a privilege to be able to share our home with a pet. But it requires not only the initial expense of purchasing an animal but also the ongoing commitment of time and money to interact with it and care for it prop-

erly. Too often rescue groups or humane society workers are asked to find another home for a pet because its owner has grown bored with it or is unable to afford its care.

The Selection Process

Rats are very social animals. Living in colonies, their behaviors include mutual grooming, sharing common sleeping areas, play, and caring for the young. Whenever possible, pet rats should also be kept at least in pairs, preferably of the same sex and approximately the same age. If you plan to have only one rat, you should spend a significant amount of time interacting with it: holding, stroking, feeding, and supervising its exploration. While it isn't mandatory to keep more than one, it is a more natural way of life and a significantly better quality of life for the animal.

As a rule, you should adopt or buy young rats that are approximately 4 or 5 weeks old. A young rat is much easier to socialize and

TIP

Avoiding Fights

Rats may fight with one another, and when they do they can cause serious injury. Overcrowding leads to stress and fighting, so make sure your pets' habitat is large enough to give all the occupants plenty of space. Be sure to provide enough hiding places (hide-boxes, tunnel tubes) for your rats. Female rats may fight when they are in estrus or if they have babies. Female rats with babies need two to four times more space (depending on litter size) than female rats without offspring. Male rats are more prone to fighting when they are in the presence of a female rat and to attempt to establish dominance or protect territory or food. Neutering (surgical castration) can help reduce aggressive behavior. Male rats that are siblings or that have been raised together from a very young age are less likely to quarrel.

tame than a mature one. You should bear this in mind especially if you are purchasing rats at a pet store, since the store employees rarely have time to get the animals accustomed to handling by humans. This is not the case for rats purchased from a breeder, as most breeders handle their rats often.

There is little difference between male and female rats with respect to learning ability and capacity for affection. When young, both sexes quickly adapt to being carried, stroked, and hand-fed. They are equally inquisitive and eager to explore every nook and cranny. You should house pairs or groups of males separate from females to prevent unwanted litters. Segregated groups usually get along well as long

as they are approximately the same age and the enclosure or habitat is of adequate size.

Quarantining New Rats

Every new rat that you acquire should be isolated from the rats you currently own. New rats should be quarantined for a minimum of two weeks. Put the new rat or rats into a separate habitat so you can watch them for signs of disease.

If you purchase two or more new rats from the same source, you don't need to put each one into its own cage; one is sufficient. All of the necessary daily care—feeding, watering, cleaning out the habitat, and playtime—for your existing rats should be done before the same care is given to the new ones to prevent disease transmission from the new rats.

If *any* of your rats appears to be sick, don't allow it to mingle with the other rats—even after the isolation period. These precautions

help to prevent the spread and minimize the severity of disease in a rat colony. Failure to quarantine new rats leads to rapid spread of an illness, just as cold germs spread through a classroom of children.

Introducing New Rats

Rats are social animals that enjoy each others' company, so it is best to house them in groups of two or more. A rat that lives alone is a very bored and lonely rat! Rats are active during the night, so make sure that your rats have each other to groom, cuddle, and play with while you are sleeping! If you have a large enough habitat for three rats, that is ideal, so that when one of the animals eventually dies, there are still two animals remaining to keep each other company.

If you have acquired a new rat, be sure to introduce it to your other rat(s) slowly and

TIP

Rat Communication
Rats communicate in many ways:
1. Sense of smell and olfactory signals
2. Tactile communication, sense of touch
3. Sounds, hearing, vocalizations
4. Body language

carefully and do not leave your rats alone together until you know they are compatible and will not fight.

Young rats are easiest to introduce and less likely to fight. An adult male rat may behave aggressively toward a younger male and not accept him. Male rats can be very protective of territory and food and fight to establish dominance.

You can begin introductions by placing your newcomer's cage alongside your established pet's cage. This way they can smell, hear, and see one another, but cannot harm each other. Over time, if your rats appear to have accepted each other's presence through the cage bars, you may begin introductions on neutral territory outside of the animals' home cages. *Do not put your new rat in your established rat's cage!*

Create "neutral territory" by placing fresh, unused litter or bedding in a thoroughly washed caged that does not contain the odors of any other rats. Another option is to enclose a small area where the animals cannot climb out or fall, and place a clean cloth on the surface and carefully introduce the animals to each other. *Supervise your rats at all times and do not leave them alone.* Watch them

carefully for signs of compatibility. They will initially circle one another, sniff, lick, investigate, and hopefully accept each other. *If they start to fight, separate them immediately.* Be careful! Do not risk being bitten if your rats are fighting. Use a tube to separate them. Don't use your hands or fingers!

T I P

Signs of Stress in Rats
1. Circling
2. Repetitive behavior, such as pacing
3. Bar chewing
4. Weight loss
5. Teeth chattering or grinding

HOW-TO: SELECTING A

The most common source for pet rats is a pet store. Many pet stores keep rats in stock and sell them for $4 to $6. Most of these rats are considered "feeders" because they are sold primarily as food for captive reptiles, such as snakes and some carnivorous (meat-eating) lizards and birds. They may be of unknown age, but they are probably going to be hooded or albinos (pink-eyed whites, or PEWs). Depending on the animal's age, the feelings that the pet store staff has toward rats, and the amount of free time the staff has, pet store rats may or may not be very socialized. Most will be apprehensive about being touched but will accept food gratefully if gently coaxed. Some will be frightened either because of improper handling, like being picked up by the tail or from lack of socialization. These rats can often be rehabilitated with patience and experienced hands. Pet stores purchase rats from community breeders or from wholesale retailers. If your local pet store does not stock rats, it may be willing to order one for you.

Breeders

Purchasing from a pet store usually does not offer the advantage of selecting a rat based on its appearance or personality; you need to contact a breeder for this. Fortunately, this is becoming easier. Rats purchased from a reputable breeder are going to be more socialized and healthier than rats from a pet store, where frequent introduction of new stock and stress of constant scrutiny predisposes them to disease.

If you are willing to shop around, you will have your choice of a wide variety of coat color and pattern. Be prepared to pay more for fancy rats, usually $15 to $30 per animal. If you choose a breeder located some distance from your home, you will have to arrange for transportation too. Many breeders will ship animals by air at your expense. Regulations governing shipment of animals vary among airlines and states or countries.

Good breeders:
✔ Maintain strict sanitation practices.
✔ Quarantine new breeding stock and animals that they have taken to shows.
✔ Keep records.
✔ Remove from the breeding program animals that are sick, produce offspring with birth defects, high disease incidence, or aggressive behavior.
✔ Socialize their animals to being handled.
✔ Interview people who purchase their animals and place their rats in suitable, loving homes.

Rescue Groups

There are rat rescue groups that work to place unwanted pets into new homes. Most of these rats are adult animals

PET RAT

whose owners have grown bored with them, or may no longer be able to keep them because of allergies, other pets, moving, and so forth. They will vary in their socialization and ability to adapt to a new environment. You may be asked to make a donation to the rescue group in exchange for one of these rats.

Additional Sources

You can locate breeders and rescue groups through:

1. Rat clubs have members that breed for hobby and profit. They are listed on the club's Internet web pages as links, or make themselves known on the club's bulletin boards, forums, and published newsletters. (See Information on page 92.)

2. Newspapers/pet magazines list pets for sale in the classified section.

3. The Internet has many web pages maintained by people who love rats. It's a good place to network.

4. Rat shows attract everyone—from those people with a casual interest in keeping rats to the devotee. Here is a good place to meet breeders face-to-face, and to talk with and find out about some of your concerns.

5. Other rat fanciers may recommend a source that they consider to be reputable.

6. Veterinarians who care for rats may be able to direct your search.

7. Humane societies often take in unusual pets or know local individuals who are willing to provide foster care for unwanted rats that would otherwise be euthanized until a permanent home can be found.

What to Look For

Before purchasing any rat from a group, observe the rats for any physical condition that

may suggest a health problem. The fur should be uniform and free of bald spots, wounds, and flaky skin. A rat should not limp or hold a paw or leg abnormally while walking or sitting. The corners of the eyes and the nose should be free of discharge or brownish-red discoloration. A rat's head should be held upright, not tipped to one side. Listen for any sneezing and look at the character of the droppings in the cage. They should be formed, not puddled in a corner.

Also look carefully at the cages where the animals are housed. Are the habitats clean? Does the food and water look fresh? If you are considering purchasing a rat from a pet store, ask about the source of the rats, how long they have been at the store, and their approximate age. You should not purchase an animal that has been kept in a dirty cage or one that shows any signs of respiratory disease or diarrhea. Nor should you purchase a rat that has been housed with other sick animals. Poor husbandry predisposes the rat to diseases that may show up after you take it home.

SUPPLIES AND HOUSING

Unless you are directly supervising your rat's exploration and playtime, you should keep your friend in an escape-proof enclosure. You can buy rodent habitats at a pet store and through online retailers. Most people choose either a wire cage or glass aquarium. Both types of habitat have advantages and disadvantages.

Habitats

You can build a habitat using your own design and materials, but make sure the structure that you build is sturdy enough to house a rat. Multilevel habitats may appear more interesting to you than the single-level variety; however, a food dish and several toys reduce the space significantly. I recommend that a habitat for a single rat be no smaller than say a 10-gallon (40-L) aquarium. More animals need more space, so use common sense.

Cages vary in size, bed spacing, shape, and number of tiers or levels connected by ladders or ramps. Many people buy ferret cages because of their size and enriched environment. They are lightweight, and because they can be scrubbed with a brush, rinsed, and left to air-dry, they are easy to keep clean. Cages provide good ventilation so bedding stays drier and ammonia levels stay low. A cage is fairly escape-proof, provided its door is latched securely and the wires are close together. Wire spacing should be ½ inch (1.3 cm) to avoid injury if a leg or foot is caught between the wires.

But cages have negative aspects as well. Over time, the acids in the animals' urine corrode cages. Galvanized steel cages contain the metal zinc, which can be toxic if ingested. Powder-coated or plastic-coated cages prevent this potential risk. Another problem with housing rats in cages is that the rats can develop large foot calluses from climbing and standing on the wire surfaces. When these calluses become infected with painful sores, the condition is called "bumblefoot."

To prevent foot problems, the cage floor should be lined with a removable piece of Plexiglas. A hardware store can cut a piece of Plexiglas to size for you. Plexiglas is superior to other materials because it's sturdy, easy to clean, and nontoxic. Plastic mesh canvas, found in craft supply departments or stores, is another good product for flooring. Urine and other debris move through the holes keeping the floor cleaner and drier. Plastic mesh should be scrubbed thoroughly to remove any material trapped in the tiny holes.

Avoid using pieces of wood, as wood floors soak up urine and are difficult to disinfect. Wood also splinters, and the slivers can find their way into your rat's feet. Your rat is likely to chew up a wood floor, too. Cardboard floors tend to become mushy from urine, and promote the growth of germs.

Depending on the brand, size, number of tiers and accessories, wire cages start at about $40 for a basic model adequate for one or two rats. Tall, multilevel cages with tubes and hammocks can cost more than $250. Avoid single-level cages marketed for hamsters and mice. These are inexpensive, but are too small for even one rat.

A Plexiglas or glass aquarium is one housing option for your pet rat. The aquarium should be at least 20 gallon size and large enough to accommodate a large exercise wheel, nesting area, and feeding area. The smooth flooring is easy on the rat's feet, and you don't have to worry about zinc poisoning. Pet stores sell clip-on wire tops for most standard size aquariums that prevent rats from escaping.

Unfortunately, aquariums are heavy and can be cumbersome to clean. If you drop your aquarium, it may break. Although an aquarium's clear sides allow easy viewing of your pet, the ventilation in an aquarium is very limited.

Temperature and humidity are higher inside an aquarium because it retains body heat and vapor moisture from the animals. Urine, feces, and food material in the bedding make an ideal place for bacteria to grow. As bacteria grow in the soiled bedding, ammonia gas is produced. Ammonia irritates the rat's delicate respiratory tract, which can lead to severe, and sometimes fatal, pneumonia. For that reason, you must make sure the aquarium is always clean.

Plastic cages called Habitrails, which consist of a series of chambers connected by tunnels, are suitable for smaller rodents like hamsters and mice, but are too small for an adult rat. Some of the larger and more expensive ferret cages come equipped with plastic tunnels large enough for most rats.

Bedding

Bedding material should absorb the rat's waste and control odor. An ideal bedding is dust-free, absorbent, lightweight, and free of harmful pesticides and resins. It also should be environmentally safe, inexpensive, and easily obtainable. Several bedding materials are avail-

able, none of which meets all these criteria. Bedding material is not the same as nesting material, which is loose material provided for tunneling and warmth.

Paper and wood are the two basic bedding products. Both products are manufactured in shreds (or shavings) and pellets. Each product has its own benefits and drawbacks. Several companies manufacture pelleted paper products. The basic ingredient in all of them is recycled newspaper. It is dust-free, absorbent, biodegradable, and compostable. Many companies claim their products are flushable, at least in small quantities, but this is not recommended for septic systems. Pelleted paper is reasonably priced. Some people dislike this product because it isn't very soft on the rat's feet. Odor control is not as good as with some other products and the pellets break down when wet. These disadvantages vary depending on the manufacturer, and as with most products, some are better than oth-

Shavings

If you prefer to use shavings in your rat's habitat, aspen shavings are recommended. They do not contain the aromatic substances found in cedar and pine shavings that can cause itchy skin and liver or respiratory problems. Some pine shavings have been processed to eliminate undesirable resins and oils, so check the packaging. Always use only shavings that are packaged and indicated for direct-contact use as bedding material for caged pets. Do not use shavings that are sold for horse stalls or stored in open outdoor bins. They may be contaminated by feces and urine of wild rats and can pose a health problem for your rat.

Bedding Choices

Bedding Type	Products	Advantages	Disadvantages
Paper (pelleted, recycled newspapers, shredded paper)	Yesterday's news Marshall's Ferret Litter Cell-Sorb Plus Eco-bedding Homemade	Not dusty, absorbent, biodegrades, flushable, nontracking, moderately priced, readily available, good odor control, compostable	Coarse, mushy when wet
Wood (aspen, pine, wood pulp)	Care Fresh Aspen Fresh Kaytee	Absorbent, smells good, good odor control, biodegrades, compostable, readily available	Can be dusty, expensive; pine products should be processed to remove resins and oils
Miscellaneous (cloth, corncob, wheat products)	Felt Old T-shirts Swheat Scoop Critter Country	Can be inexpensive and recyclable	Can be expensive, poor odor control, can have limited availability, "ringtail"

ers. You should try several brands and decide for yourself.

Shredded paper is another choice for bedding or litter. You can make shredded paper yourself using clean, recyclable paper and an inexpensive paper shredder. There are also commercially available shredded paper products. This bedding can be very economical if you make it yourself from office paper waste or brown grocery bags. It is soft and warm and dust-free, and can be delightfully fun for the rats as they tunnel through it. Shredded paper also serves as nesting material. Unfortunately, shredded paper isn't very absorbent and it doesn't control odor very well. The ink from the paper can transfer onto the rat's fur, and some inks are toxic to rats.

Sterilized wood shavings traditionally have been the most commonly used products for rat bedding. Cedar shavings, and to a lesser extent pine shavings, are not recommended because of the phenols and resins that give them their pungent fragrance. Phenols and resins are toxic to the respiratory tract and predispose the animals to liver damages, as well as infection.

Several pelleted wood products made from recycled wood pulp and aspen are an excellent choice for rat bedding. They are absorbent, biodegradable, and compostable, and again are reported to be flushable in small amounts. Aspen pellets can be somewhat dusty, but they smell good. Pellet products are sometimes made from pine, but most are not. The biggest disadvantages of pelleted wood products are price and texture. They tend to be fairly costly and although there are differences between brands, they can be rough on the rat's feet.

Processed corncob and cloth are less common choices for bedding. Processed corncob tends to be less available and more expensive than wood or paper bedding products. It should not be used for nursing mothers and weanlings during dry winter months because it has been associated with a condition called "ringtail."

Ringtail is a lesion on young rats characterized by annular (circular, or ringlike) constrictions on the tail. The tissue of the tail can die, and the affected part of the tail may fall off. This problem is associated with low humidity (less than 40 percent) and also with prolonged temperatures of 80°F (26.6°C) and higher. Cloth material, such as felt or jersey, can be used for bedding. They are soft and absorbent and can be washed and used again if desired. Cloth is not good for odor control. Don't use terry cloth towels or other fabric that unravels as the fibers catch on the rat's feet and toes, and cause injury.

Litter Box

Rats can be litter box trained (see chapter on Training). The cage that you choose may have a litter box accessory, usually a corner-shaped unit, or be a rectangular, low-sided container, such as a small food storage container.

Nesting Box

Your rat needs some type of bed, either a nest it creates for itself out of loose bedding material, such as shredded paper or batting, or a box or tube for privacy. Many people like to give their rats a suspended hammock for snuggling and sleeping.

Containers for Food and Water

To help keep your rat's food clean, put it into a heavy, non-spill, ceramic crock or non-tip bowl. Do not use plastic containers because rats chew on them. Small plastic pieces may cause choking or gastrointestinal obstruction in your pet.

Rats can climb into their food dishes and urinate and defecate, so be sure to empty and clean your pet's food dish daily and replace it with fresh food. Remove any leftover perishable food from the habitat every day so that it doesn't spoil and cause a health problem. Your rats will probably hide favorite food morsels in the bedding, so check there as well.

Provide your pet with fresh water daily in a bottle suspended from the side of the habitat. Use only metal sipper tubes. Do not use bottles with plastic sipper tubes because your rat can chew and break the sipper tubes. Always check the sipper tube daily to be sure it is working properly and that it is not plugged.

Suspend the water bottle high enough so that it does not come in contact with bedding material or wick out into the bedding.

The water will stay clean of bedding material and excrement, and doesn't spill as easily as it would in a bowl. These bottles also prevent the water from evaporating, which is a handy feature if you have to leave your rat alone for a day or two.

TIP

Water Bottle Basics
✔ Always be sure to tighten the cap of a water bottle securely before you turn the bottle upside down!
✔ Always check the sipper tube to be sure it is not plugged!
✔ You should purchase two bottles and alternate them every day.
✔ Scrub the bottle with a brush in hot soapy water and let it air-dry, replacing it in the habitat with a clean one.

Feed Fresh Food

Be sure the food you give your rats is fresh! Although it is tempting to buy in bulk to save money, if you buy more food than your rat can eat in a reasonable time, the food will lose freshness. Do not feed food that is older than six months from the time of milling. When the food package has been opened, vitamins in the food lose their potency and are no longer effective.

Toys

Outside of their own company, you will be your rats' major source of entertainment, but you can provide toys for amusement when you're not available. Small blocks of wood and cardboard tubes suitable for chewing, small boxes, wire wheels, ropes for climbing, ladders, and ramps are all good toys.

Use your imagination to design and build a maze with your rat's favorite food reward at the end. Then see how quickly your rat learns to negotiate the pattern. Mazes can be built with PVC pipe, boxes, and cardboard tubes. Most rats enjoy swimming. Use a small tub with tepid water and never leave your rat unattended in the "pool."

Remember that a rat's teeth grow continuously, and grind down when chewing food and by gnawing on objects. Make sure that wood blocks are not pressure-treated with chemicals. Don't use hamster balls with your rat. "Hamster balls" are popular toys used for exercising other small pets like hamsters and gerbils. They are clear balls that separate into two pieces. The pet is placed inside and the ball is reassembled and placed on the floor. The pet then runs freely while being confined inside the ball.

These toys are dangerous because the animal can easily overheat inside the ball due to poor ventilation.

The Cost of a Rat and Supplies

A rat purchased from a pet store costs about $10; fancy rats cost up to $50. Plan to spend a minimum of $50 to $100 for an aquarium or no-frills cage. Very nice, multiple tiered cages start at around $175, and a wire cover for an aquarium costs about $15. A small crock food bowl, two sipper bottles, and hanging rack runs about $15 to $20. Ongoing expenses include those for food and bedding material. All together, the expense to set up your rat and home is about $150, if you buy all new supplies.

You might be able to find a bargain on deluxe accommodations for your pet by searching through the classified ads in your local paper or rat club newsletters, and on web sites for used pet supplies, or by checking garage sales.

T I P

Safe Chew Sticks

Some people use twigs as chew sticks for their pet rats; however, some trees can be toxic for rats. Make sure all chew sticks you give your pet are safe! You can purchase safe chew sticks for your rat from your local pet store.

CARING FOR RATS

The type and size of your rat's habitat, the bedding and sanitation, the number of animals you house together, and the way you feed them are all part of what is collectively termed husbandry. Aside from genetics, your rat's health, longevity, and quality of life are directly related to two important factors: the quality of your husbandry and your attention to nutrition.

Preparing for Your Rat's Arrival

Close, cramped quarters, dirty bedding, temperature extremes, drafts, excessive noise and lights, and poor nutrition are some of the stress factors that predispose all animals to disease. The subject of nutrition is discussed at some length in another section of this book. Here are some guidelines for good husbandry practices.

The optimal environmental temperature for rats is between 65° and 80°F (18° and 26°C). Locate the cage or aquarium away from open windows and other spots where there are drafts or intense direct sunlight that cause drastic temperature changes throughout the day.

The lighting in the habitat should be dim to moderate. Too much light can cause damage to the retina, or light-sensitive tissue at the back of the eyes. This is especially true of albino rats, which lack pigment in the iris. The iris is the colored part of the eye with a hole in the center called the pupil. In bright light, the pupil gets smaller to block out intense light from reaching the retina. The pupil, together with the pigment in the iris, act like built-in sunglasses to protect the retina.

Relative humidity in the rat's habitat should be maintained between 50 and 70 percent. Low humidity conditions, (see pages 33–34) damage the rat's respiratory tract, and are responsible for the disease "ringtail." The drying effect of your furnace and some bedding materials—particularly processed corncob—all rob the air of moisture and contribute to these health problems. You can increase the moisture level in the air by using a room humidifier.

Your First Days Home

You should have everything ready—the habitat, bedding, food and bowl, and water bottle—and in place when you bring your rat home for the first time. At first, place the cage or aquarium in a spot that is away from the household center of activity. Later, when your rat is accustomed to the environment and to being handled, you can move the habitat to a busier part of the household.

It's a good idea not to handle a new rat too much the first day. The new sights, sounds, and smells can be frightening. In the wild, rats eat, sleep, and reproduce in a small territory, although they travel long distances for food if necessary. Allow your rat to explore, rearrange, and mark its new home with urine for most of the first day. Watch his exploration and speak softly until the rat becomes familiar with your voice.

After a short time, you can begin to put your hand into the cage or aquarium for your rat to sniff. Most likely, the rat will scurry away rather than approach you. If you offer small tidbits of food, the rat will learn that your presence promises something tasty and good. You will gain your rat's trust much more quickly if you feed it exclusively by hand.

How to Pick Up a Rat

In a short time, your rat won't run away from your hand, but toward it! A rat is motivated by the promise of food, of course, but this will soon change to affection. Remember never to pick up your rat by the tail! If suspended in midair this way, a rat will paddle its feet and twist its body to find footing. A very young rat, or one unaccustomed to being handled, may, out of panic, fear, and potentially pain, try to bite you. Instead, to pick up a rat, slide your hand under its belly.

A new young rat may sit quietly frightened in your cupped hand. He may circle tightly or lick you. Some rats will try to jump away or crawl along your arm heading for your shoulder or folds in your clothes. If your new rat has been very active, you should anticipate an escape attempt and be sure that you are sitting down to prevent falls or jumps. Be sure that room doors are closed and other pets are out of the area.

Rat Restraint

Occasionally it will be necessary to immobilize your rat—to give medication or to make an examination, for example. To do this, gather up the loose skin behind the back of the neck (called the "scruff") between your thumb and forefinger, and suspend the rat upright and cradled in your hand. Rats that have been handled often usually do not struggle; if it does put up a fight, you may have to hold the back feet.

Some rats twist and struggle and really object to being "scruffed." If your pet struggles, wrap it snugly in a small towel with only its head exposed. To do this, lay the towel on a flat surface and place the rat's neck along the long edge. Extend the front legs back and at the same time, wrap one end of the towel snugly against its body to prevent the front legs from reaching forward. Then, bring the other end of the towel up and overlap the body. The towel should be wide enough to cover the rat's rear feet. You have to be quick with this because determined rats can slip their front legs out of the towel and wiggle out of your grasp. Immobilizing the front feet is really the key to success here.

Don't wrap your rat so tightly that its chest is compressed and breathing is restricted. Once immobilized, you should be able to administer oral medication, eye drops, or ointments. You may be able to restrain a foot and trim the nails, too.

Housekeeping

A dirty habitat can lead to severe health problems for your pet, as well as unpleasant odors. How frequently you should clean the cage or aquarium depends on how messy your

rat is with its food, the type of bedding used, the number of rats in the habitat, and the amount of waste that is produced.

If you have only one or two rats, all the bedding should be removed and the habitat scrubbed clean and rinsed at least once a week. You don't need to buy or use anything special for cleaning; hot, soapy water made with dishwashing soap will do. Some abrasives and cleaners cause plastic and Plexiglas to turn cloudy. Even worse, some household cleaning products can be very toxic to rats. Residues in the cage or aquarium can vaporize and cause damage to a rat's internal organs and respiratory tract. So be sure to rinse all traces of cleaners from the surfaces of the habitat. Should you need a disinfectant, a diluted bleach solution (3 percent) is an excellent one. Soak surfaces with diluted bleach solution for 10 minutes, then rinse throughly.

In between cleanings, remove the wet bedding and replace it with fresh bedding material as needed. Your rats will choose one area of the

TIP

Possible Hazards

✔ other pets
✔ falling from heights
✔ falling objects
✔ open doors and windows
✔ electrical cords and outlets
✔ cleaning agents and other chemicals
✔ drugs in the medicine cabinet
✔ pesticides and herbicides
✔ alcoholic beverages
✔ caffeine
✔ recliners and convertible furniture
✔ clothes dryers, refrigerators
✔ mousetraps
✔ sharp objects in trash
✔ rancid garbage
✔ automobile exhaust fumes
✔ crevices in walls
✔ plastic bags
✔ being stepped upon
✔ swinging doors
✔ toilets, aquariums, and other containers with water
✔ wood stoves and fireplaces
✔ portable heaters
✔ most houseplants

habitat to deposit most of the urine and fecal waste. Rats can be trained to use a litter box, too. Rats also like to hide their favorite foods in bedding and nesting

material, so be sure to remove old food daily to prevent spoilage.

Food and water containers should be emptied and thoroughly cleaned every day. Use a bottlebrush to remove bacterial film from the inside surface of the bottles. Again, hot, soapy water made with dishwashing soap is just fine. Don't add vitamin supplements or other substances to the drinking water unless your veterinarian has specifically prescribed them. Vitamins added to water promote the growth of bacteria in the bottles.

Rats and Other Pets

Not everyone or every creature in your household will enjoy your pet rat in the same way you do. Cats and dogs are natural predators of rats and should not be left unsupervised in the presence of your rat when it is outside of its habitat. The same advice holds for hungry snakes.

Small children naturally take to animals. To most children, rats are simply curious, furry bundles that feel nice against the skin. Very young children may not realize that rough handling can injure a rat or provoke it to bite. And, of course, there are children who intentionally mistreat small animals. Be sure to

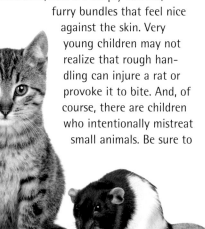

discuss how to handle and play with a rat with the little people in your household.

Rats are not domesticated to anywhere near the degree that other companion animals are. The more you interact with your rat, the more trusting and tame it will become. Eventually, you may find your rat curled up on your shoulder or in your pocket while you read.

Free Range Rats

Many people involved in rat fancy allow their rats to roam freely in their homes some of the time. This certainly integrates the ratties into the home and family more in the way we do our dog and cat pets, and permits us to appreciate their individual personalities. In the lexicon of rat fanciers, a group of rats is called a "mischief" for a very good reason. By nature, they are explorers. Rats can't distinguish between the appropriateness of gnawing on electrical cords, your expensive athletic shoes, or the cardboard tube left in their cage as a toy. It's impossible to discipline a rat to leave wires, furniture, carpeting, papers, or anything of value alone. You must "rat proof" the environment for your pet's safety.

Although your rat may be litter box trained and may deposit most of its waste into the habitat, your rat still will deposit urine and feces wherever it wanders. Rats also spray urine on vertical surfaces as cats do. This is how both male and female rats mark territory. That means you, your clothing, your bed, couch, other upholstered furniture, and rugs are going to be marked with urine. Over time, and with more rats, the amount of urine can become significant, and you should anticipate the need to have furniture and rugs cleaned to prevent rodent odor. Consider covering any absorbent surfaces with something that can be removed and laundered easily.

Transporting Your Rat

From time to time, it may be necessary for you to take your rat on a brief excursion outside the home—to the veterinary hospital, to a friend's house, or to a classroom, for example. You can purchase a small rodent carrier made of clear, easy-to-clean plastic, with a vented

rail, you should inquire about the policy for transporting pets. Most airlines allow small animals in the cabin, provided the carrier fits under the seat in front of you. There is usually a limit of one animal in the cabin per flight.

On long trips, you can transport a rat directly in its habitat. If this is not practical, a cat carrier equipped with a handle and wire door may serve your purposes. Be sure to bring along plenty of bedding and food for your entire trip, unless you know that there will be a place to purchase these supplies at your destination.

Many rat fanciers prefer to make their own carrying cases and travel containers for their pets. These carrier cases are inexpensive and easy to make. Start by purchasing plastic file boxes from your local office supply store. For a secure lid, cut out the center of the plastic lid that came with the file box and replace it with wire mesh (see photo). You can also use hard plastic mesh, the kind used for placing under tiles, available from your local hardware supply store (see photo). You can make a hole for the water bottle attachments and sipper tube by using a wood burner or similiar tool to make a smooth, small hole in the plastic without cracking it.

What About Your Vacation?

One of the nice things about having a pet rat is that you can leave it unattended while you go away on a day trip. Just be sure to provide enough food and fresh water for your pet. Hang a second sipper-tube bottle on the cage, just to be safe.

If you must leave home for longer than a day, you should make arrangements for your

top and handle. There's not much room inside one of these carriers, so don't plan on using one for a long trip.

Longer trips require more preparation if you plan to bring along your rat—a move to another apartment or house, or an extended vacation, for instance. If you are traveling by car, your only concern is how the hotel will receive your rat. If you are traveling by air or

TIP

Car Safety

Remember that during the summer months the inside of your car can become extremely hot in a very short time, even with a window cracked open. Never leave your rat, or any other animal, in a car in hot weather. If you are traveling in the wintertime, take your rat with you when you leave the car. Hypothermia is just as deadly as overheating.

pet to be cared for in your absence. Perhaps a friend would be willing to look after your rat. If this is not possible, consider contacting a boarding facility for animals. The facility probably has few requests for rat-sitting services and may be willing to look after your unusual pet—for a fee, of course. Some veterinary hospitals provide this service too, or have staff members who look after pets at home.

If you decide that you'd rather take your rat with you, consider the stresses involved for the rat. You may conclude that even a new environment and having a stranger provide its care is far less stressful for your rat.

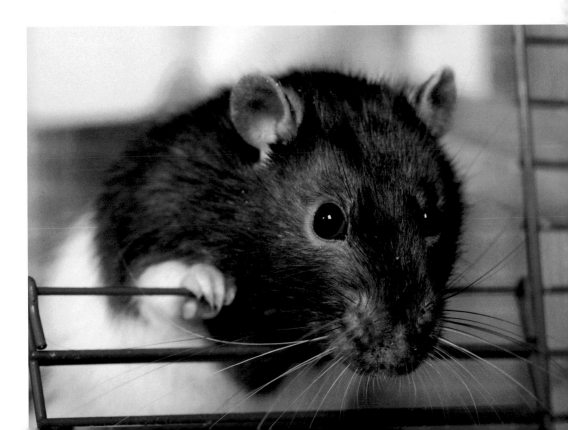

TRAINING

One of the most appealing characteristics of domestic rats is their curiosity about— and their willingness to interact with—humans. Rats learn to trust their natural adversaries—cats, dogs, and humans—and seek them out.

An Endearing Pet

Rats are curious and love to explore outside their habitat, rather than hide. They become comfortable being turned on their backs or carried around on shoulders. And they love to explore you too—your hair, your ears, your pockets.

Even when afraid, a pet rat is not likely to bite. Its first defense in a fearful situation is to urinate and defecate on its handler, and wriggle and writhe itself free. If possible, a rat will run for a familiar place like its cage. Contented rats grind or bruxate their teeth.

Most rats obtained as young adolescents quickly respond to gentle handling.

Establishing Trust

Your rat needs at least a day or two after arriving in your household to get over the stress of having been transported, and to adjust to its new environment: the smell of the bedding and food, the habitat, room noises,

and lights. Once your rat has had the opportunity to explore its enclosure, mark it with urine and droppings, and eat and drink, it will be less frightened of being held.

Spend at least 30 minutes to an hour each day interacting with your rat. The more time that you spend, the quicker it will "bond" with you. If you feed your rat by hand, one small tidbit at a time, it will learn to accept you even more quickly. The more bonded your rat becomes to you, the easier it will be to teach it to come when its name is called, or to do other "tricks." And the more bonded you are to each other, the more enjoyment you will have from owning a rat!

Taking Advantage of Natural Behaviors

Scientists studying behavior in rats have long used food rewards. Circus and marine animal trainers do the same. Perhaps you have visited a marine park where sea mammals leap and retrieve floats for the favor of a fish. Trainers know that the tricks these animals perform are an extension of their natural behaviors. Dolphins, for instance, love to leap out of the water. Their trainers expand on this natural behavior by rewarding them when they leap in response to a signal. Because dolphins are innately intelligent, they put two and two together very quickly and so, learn to leap on command.

Of course a rat cannot learn to fetch your slippers, but it can learn to come when called. It can learn to climb or sit up, if it is inclined to do so in its natural behavior. By observing its traits and postures and using food rewards along with signals, you can train your rat to perform certain "tricks" for you.

The most familiar example to all of us is a rat's ability to rapidly memorize the pattern of a maze or agility course. You can construct a course at home using boxes, tubes, ladders, steps, ropes, nets, and ramps. See how quickly your rat learns to navigate the course. Then redesign it and see how quickly your rat learns the new one. Compare these times with those of other rats, in an Ultimate Rat Race.

Litter Box Training

Rats can be trained to eliminate in a litter box. Choose a type of litter different from the material that you select for bedding so that the rat learns to associate that type with elimination.

As with rabbits, rats often select one or more places in the habitat where they prefer to deposit urine and feces. By watching carefully, you can identify that area or areas and put the litter boxes there. Put the rat inside the litter box so it can sniff and dig. Put some of the rat's feces into the litter box, too. If you watch the rat and actually see it eliminating in the litter box, praise it and give it a favorite food reward immediately. The more bonded your rat is to you, the more successful and quicker you will be in accomplishing this training.

Recognizing Their Names

Many people claim that they have taught their rats to come when their own name is called. People who spend a lot of time with their rat, and make them very socialized, have the most success with this. The process relies on food, of course, and not just any food, but the treats that the rats prize the most.

Put your rat in an open space without a lot of distractions. Call your rat's name, and when it comes to you, offer it a food reward. Use this particular treat only when you are training your pet. It must be something that the rat really loves. Use the same name every time you train. That means, if your rat's name is Snookers, don't use variations or endearing terms like Snookums or Snookie or Snooks.

The first time your rat comes to you will be by chance. If you are consistent, it should soon learn that the sound that you are making means something REALLY good and that it should come to you. You should reward your pet every time it comes. Eventually you can skip the food reward

and give a "social" reward, like petting or scratching. You don't have to use a name or even your voice to train a rat to come on command. You can use a clicker or a shaker or a bell.

What Not to Expect

There are some things you cannot expect from your rat. Rats cannot be housebroken. Even if they are successfully trained to use a litter box, they will still mark territory with urine and feces. Nor can they be trained not to chew furniture, electrical cords, or anything else in their way for that matter. Except when put off by a strong smell or frightening sound, rats explore anywhere they can. No matter how much you love your rat and think it is bonded to you, don't expect it to come to you on command every time or in every situation. Rats cannot and should not be disciplined through physical force; to do so would be cruel and inhumane. Instead, training should consist of positive reinforcement of desired behavior.

NUTRITION AND FEEDING

The success of rodents as a whole, and of rats in particular, can be largely attributed to their ability to adapt to a wide variety of circumstances, such as climate, harborage, population density, and food supply. A common rodent pet, the gerbil, lives naturally in the heat of the desert. The lemming, famous for its mass migrations, is found in the cold arctic tundra.

Feeding Habits of Wild Rats

Common brown and black rats found in nature have allied themselves with humans, living in and around buildings and dwellings, in sewers and drainpipes, in abandoned junk, and in waste disposal sites. They are common among the docks and warehouses of harbor areas where water, shelter, and food are plentiful. Rat populations spread with people—as freeloaders in sailor's larders, for example. Where there are people, there are also rats.

The number of rats in any colony depends on the site of the habitat they have invaded, the amount of fresh water available and, most important, the food supply. Rats become more aggressive with one another when food is scarce. Some rats leave the colony to start a new one where there is more food.

Wild rats consume just about anything to survive. But, like most creatures, they prefer to eat what is easiest and most accessible.

Food Preferences

Rats have food preferences! Pest exterminator companies have capitalized on these preferences to reduce the rat populations in human habitats. Rat poisons are sometimes prepared as pellets that can be carried back to the burrow and shared with the rest of the colony.

Wild rats spend their nights scavenging for food. They eat seeds, nuts, berries, fruits, and eggs from nests, and the unprotected young of other animals and birds. They invade silos and bins to eat grains stored for seed or for feeding livestock.

City rats scour cans and dump sites for edible garbage and raid human dwellings for food. They leave behind damaged grain bags and containers, droppings, urine, and hair. If they are hungry, they may consume their plunder on the spot, but they usually carry or drag it back to the burrow before eating it. You will see your pet rats doing this too, as they usually remove choice foods from the bowl and hide it in bedding.

Not all of the food that is brought into a rat nest is consumed. Some of it may go rancid, and will be eaten only if the supply of fresh food is limited. Rats that become ill, but do not die from consuming rancid food or poisoned bait, will shy away from the same foods later on. Your pet rat is no exception; it can quickly learn to avoid "off" or tainted foods, such as those laced with unpleasant medication.

According to the National Academy of Sciences, rats—or for that matter, all animals—have five basic nutritional requirements:

✔ energy
✔ proteins
✔ fats
✔ vitamins
✔ minerals

A deficiency in any single requirement prevents all the others from performing their duties. Let's look at each requirement—what it is made of, its function, and how it is fulfilled in the diet.

Energy and Carbohydrates

The energy or fuel needed for growth, healing, repair, and reproduction is derived mostly from carbohydrates, such as starches and sugars. Proteins and fats can also be used for energy, but this is not their only function. The amount of energy contained in any food is measured in terms of calories. A calorie is sim-

Increased Demands for Energy

Other rat activities that require additional energy are gestation and lactation. The mother eats to support her own body's needs and those of the pups developing inside the uterus. The female rat increases her food consumption by 25 to 50 percent to meet those needs. Extra energy is also needed during recovery from illness or trauma, or in cold weather to stay warm if animals are exposed to these conditions.

ply the amount of heat that is given off when a substance is burned. In the laboratory, scientists measure the calorie content of foods by burning a precise amount and then measuring the heat that is released in the process.

Carbohydrates and proteins of all kinds produce the same amount of heat, and thus have the same caloric contents. One gram of a carbohydrate or protein contains four calories. Fats contain far more; one gram of fat contains nine calories of energy, more than twice that of carbohydrates and proteins. It's easy to see why people hoping to lose weight should avoid eating fatty foods. Likewise, it's easy to understand that for a thin animal to gain weight, it needs added dietary fat, not proteins or carbohydrates, to accomplish this most efficiently.

Most of the rat's motivation for obtaining food comes from its need for energy. The amount of energy, and therefore calories, a rat needs depends on its life-cycle stage. Rats require more energy during their rapid growth phase—from birth to approximately three to four months of age. After that time, their rate

of growth slows and they don't need as many calories to sustain their tissues and provide energy for daily activity. Naturally, if your rat is athletically inclined and gets a lot of exercise, it will need more calories each day than a rat with a more sedentary lifestyle.

Energy comes primarily from the carbohydrates found in grains such as oats, barley, wheat, milo, quinoa, and rice. Vegetables like beans, corn, alfalfa, and peas contain carbohydrates in the form of starches and sugars, as do nuts and seeds. Inside the rat's body, these foods are broken down and converted into a sugar called glucose, which is the primary fuel used for energy.

Without enough energy-producing foods, your rat will feel tired and lethargic. Energy

deprived young rats fail to grow; older animals lose weight and fail to reproduce. Severely energy deprived animals die from malnutrition or disease.

Proteins

Living creatures also require proteins in their diet. Proteins are long molecules made up of smaller ones linked together, called amino acids. When proteins are consumed, the processes of chewing and digestion break down the links between these amino acids. The amino acids are then absorbed by the body and rebuilt into the proteins of tissues, bones, nerves, hormones, blood, and other body fluids. Excess amino acids, not needed for body proteins, are further transformed and used for energy or stored as fat.

Dietary proteins come from plants and meat. Plants like grains, leguminous beans, corn, seeds, and nuts all contain proteins, because

plants need proteins to form tissues. No single plant contains proteins with a full complement of all the different kinds of amino acids needed by animals. People who are vegetarians must eat several different grains and beans to have a balanced diet. The same is true of the rat.

A minimum of 7 percent of the diet of mature rats should be protein. Rats less than 4 months of age, pregnant females, and nursing mothers require more protein—about 15 to 20 percent.

Fats

Rats don't require much fat in their diet, but they do need some. Fats are very concentrated fuel sources for energy. Gram per gram, fats provide more than twice the number of calories contained in either carbohydrates or proteins. Aside from being an excellent source of energy, fats function in the production of many hormones, and they are essential components of tissue cells.

Excess fat is stored for later use when food is scarce. Body fat stores are found inside the abdominal cavity surrounding the internal organs, inside the chest cavity surrounding the heart and great blood vessels, and in pockets under the skin and between layers of muscles. Large fat stores around organs like the heart and lungs make it difficult for them to do their job. The added weight stresses the skeleton and makes for a slow and lumbering, clumsy animal. The extra wear and tear on joints can lead to early arthritis.

Just as proteins are larger molecules made up of smaller subunits, so are fats made up of small components. The components of fats are

called fatty acids. Fatty acids are released from the fat molecule by the process of digestion, and are then absorbed into the body and put to work. Most of the fatty acids contained in foods can be manufactured by the body and need not be present in the diet at all. However, two or three fatty acids are essential—that is, it is essential that they come from a food source, because they can't be manufactured. Essential fatty acids are required in only trace amounts in the diet. But experts in rat nutrition tell us that rats grow better if there is about 5 percent fat in the diet.

Dietary fat comes from meat. It is fat that causes the "marbling effect" in roasts and steaks. Nuts and seeds also have a very high fat content. Rats, like humans, love the taste of fats in foods. Your rat may selectively pick the peanuts and sunflower seeds from a mix-ture in its bowl. If allowed to eat a diet of mostly seeds and nuts, a rat will become fat and develop deficiencies of other nutrients.

Because of the small amount required in the diet, a deficiency in the essential fatty acids is rather unlikely in a rat being fed an otherwise balanced diet. It is possible to have an essential fatty acid deficient diet—if, for example, food is stored improperly and goes rancid, destroying the fatty acids in the process. Rats deficient in fatty acids may exhibit poor hair coats, scaly skin, slow growth, or reproductive failure.

Vitamins and Minerals

Vitamins and minerals are also required in trace amounts in the diet. While glucose, amino acids, and fatty acids are the fuel and building blocks for energy and production of tissues, blood, and hormones, vitamins are required for those processes to take place. A newborn rat without vitamins in its diet is like a house builder with nails and wood, but no hammer.

Vitamins have names that describe their chemical structures but are cumbersome to pronounce. So, to make it easier to talk about them, some vitamins also have been assigned letter designations: A, D, C, E, K, and several called B. Vitamins D and C can be manufactured by the body itself (although this is not so in all animals; humans, guinea pigs, Old World monkeys, and some fruit bats cannot). Vitamins A, E, and the Bs must be included in the rat's diet. Bacteria that live in the intestinal tract make vitamin K, folic acid, and biotin.

To benefit from the bacterial synthesis of vitamins, rats, like some other animals, such as rabbits, practice coprophagy. The animal eats a significant portion of the feces, about 50 percent, and in this manner vitamins are recycled and conserved. This may sound thoroughly unpleasant, but to the rat it is very necessary to survival. In addition, in times of food scarcity, nutritional deficiencies can be avoided or delayed by recycling substances that would

otherwise be lost. Vitamins A, D, K, and E are recycled, and stored in limited amounts in the liver and fat. Vitamin A, for instance, occurring naturally in carrots, causes quite a dramatic orange color to the skin when consumed in excessive amounts.

Fruits, vegetables, nuts, and seeds are rich in minerals and vitamins, and the ingredients, called "provitamins," that the body uses to make them. By providing your rat with a variety of these foods, you will ensure that it has a full complement of necessary vitamins and minerals. Pelleted feeds, lab blocks, and grain mixtures available commercially contain all the vitamins in the necessary amounts, even those that the rat manufactures itself and those that are made by the rat's intestinal bacteria.

Vitamins and minerals are important to each of a rat's body functions: growth and maintenance of skin, bones, nerves, eyes, and all other organs; blood clotting; wound healing; release of energy; muscle contraction; nerve impulse conduction; and excretion of wastes. They even help cells to hold their shape. Keep in mind that all vitamins work together and that there can't be a deficiency in one without there being a deficiency in others. Severe vitamin deficiencies are very unlikely in rats unless the diet is extremely restricted.

Unkempt appearance, thin haircoat, scaly skin, and stunted growth all indicate a possible mild vitamin deficiency. However, these signs are also seen with many diseases, such as mange or chronic pneumonia. Your veterinarian can examine your rat and review your husbandry practices to determine how your rat's diet is affecting its overall health.

Minerals are involved in every process of an animal's body. Sodium and potassium are needed for electrical impulses to travel along

TIP

Dietary Supplements

Vitamins are subject to rapid destruction during storage and with exposure to heat and sunlight. Supplementing a commercial feed with fresh fruits and vegetables in small amounts can compensate for the loss in storage.

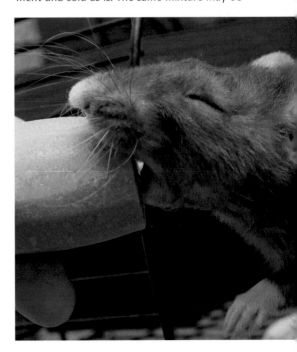

TIP

Alcohol Warning

Sadly, many people find it amusing to offer their rats an alcoholic beverage, thinking their inebriated state is somehow a "treat" for the animal. Beer, wine, liquor, or other adult beverages of choice are not suitable or appropriate libations for pets that depend on us to love and care for them. Do not give your rats alcoholic beverages.

nerves. Together with calcium, they allow muscles to contract. Calcium and phosphorus give strength to bones. Phosphorus also acts like a buffer that absorbs excess acids in the body. Your rat's body, as well as your own, uses iron to carry oxygen in the blood to tissues for metabolism. Sodium and chloride balance one another to help cells keep their shape. The mineral iodine is taken up by the thyroid gland and is incorporated into hormones. Other minerals—magnesium, copper, zinc, cobalt, and manganese, for example—assist vitamins and proteins in a variety of processes necessary for life.

Most minerals are required in the diet only in very tiny amounts. The body has elaborate methods of conserving and recycling minerals using the kidneys. Some minerals are lost in stool and urine. Excess amounts of the minerals calcium, magnesium, and phosphorus in the urine can crystallize into bladder stones.

Commercial rodent diets are supplemented with minerals, the chemical-sounding names listed at the end of the label or in the analysis

over the bulk bin at the feed store. You do not need to add them to your rat's diet.

Basic Feeding Guidelines

A trip to your pet food store can be a bewildering and enlightening outing. On the shelves you will find a number of diets labeled for hamsters, gerbils, and guinea pigs, and an occasional package marked for mice and rats. Most give the impression that they are prepared with only one or two species in mind. Any of these rodent diets is suitable for the mature rat.

Commercial diets take several forms. A mixture of grains, nuts, and seeds may be coated with a vitamin and mineral supplement and sold as is. The same mixture may be ground and extruded to form pellets or larger lab blocks. These formulations tend to be less dusty. Unlike whole-grain mixtures, pelleted feeds are 100 percent nutritionally complete in each mouthful; your rat can't pick out its favorite ingredients and leave the rest. The guaranteed analysis on the label usually gives the minimum percentages of crude protein and crude fats, and the maximum amounts of crude fiber, ash (minerals), and moisture (water) contained in the food. These numbers are approximations and do not say anything about the wholesomeness of the diet.

The wholesomeness of a commercial diet depends on the quality of the ingredients, and how the diet is manufactured and stored by the producer and supplier. Poor quality grains and other ingredients make a poor quality diet. You can't compensate by adding vitamins or putting it in attractive packaging. Heat and improper storage result in loss of nutritional value and rancidity. Slow inventory turnover can leave the diets nutritionally lacking so you must be careful about how much you buy and where you purchase them.

Rodent diets are sold by most pet and feed stores either in small, prepackaged quantities or in bulk, so you can purchase any amount that suits your needs. The prepackaged rodent diets frequently are more expensive than food sold from bulk bins. Mixed grains can cost more than pelleted feeds or lab blocks. Commercial diets vary in price, depending on the composition and packaging.

You may come across some literature on small rodent care that suggests purchasing a variety of grains in 10- or 20-pound (4.5-kg or 9-kg) sacks and then mixing your own diets. It is best to purchase commercial rodent blocks as the main part of your pets' diet. Rodent blocks are nutritionally balanced and should make up at least 80 percent of your rats' diet. Fresh vegetables and fresh fruits should make up the balance of the diet.

If you try to design a homemade diet for your rats, you risk inadvertently feeding them a diet that is not balanced or that is lacking in one or more important ingredients.

Some foods sold in pet stores and marketed for rodents include lots of seeds, grains, corn, and nuts. They also may contain rabbit pellets, which are not wholly digestible for rats. If you want to give your rat a variety, you may offer these foods, but feed them sparingly to ensure that the rodent blocks comprise the majority of your pets' diet. Otherwise, your rats will pick out only the individual pieces of food they prefer and as a result they may not have an adequate or balanced diet. In addition, corn and nuts are very fattening.

Unless you keep a large number of animals, large quantities of food probably will lose their

TIP

Storage Pointers

To be safe, buy only enough food to last for one month. After all, would you want to eat a box of cereal that's been in your pantry longer than one month? After you bring the food home:

✔ Transfer it to an airtight container.
✔ Keep it in a cool, dry place.
✔ Monitor the food for freshness. There should be no smell or visible signs of mold.

nutritional value before they can be consumed. For the average rat fancier with just a few rats, commercial diets make much more sense.

Grains, pellets, or lab blocks should be used as a food base. Supplement this base with a variety of fresh foods. Most commercial rodent diets have inadequate protein levels for growing rats under four months of age, and pregnant or nursing females. These rats should be supplemented with high-protein foods, such as cooked meats, eggs, cheese, and nuts. Wash all fruits and vegetables thoroughly before feeding them to your rat to remove hormone sprays and pesticides. Cut away all bruised or damaged portions. Do not offer your rat any moldy breads or produce. If you shouldn't eat it, your rat shouldn't either. Rats will eat virtually anything, but do not feed potato chips or other junk foods. Dog kibble and cat crunchies are high in fat. Chocolate contains a caffeine-like substance and can be poisonous to rats.

Treats abound. Pet store shelves are loaded with snacks, cakes, sticks, chews, crunchies, puffs, drops, and nibblets, all advertised as "treats" for your rat. A few are labeled as "gourmet blends," evidently for the discriminating rat. These foods are all combinations of the same ingredients found in a regular diet, although some have added molasses or fat-laden nuts, which make them very palatable to your rat's sweet tooth. These foods come in small packages at a premium price, but they should be avoided. Lots of rats love a treat of dried liver. Dog biscuits, preferably homemade, are also a good choice for an occasional "fast food" rat treat.

References used by scientific researchers specify that an adult rat consumes approximately 5 gm of food per 100 gm of body weight each

day. Rapidly growing rats, less than 5 months of age, eat twice as much. These numbers are guidlines, because a lot depends on variables, such as how much exercise a rat gets, the weather, and the composition and palatability of the diet. Feed your rat once a day. Put only as much food as will be consumed in a 24-hour period into the food bowl. Discard any leftovers before refilling the bowl. Rats are mostly nocturnal feeders; that is, they eat at night. Alternatively, you can feed your rat exclusively by hand during its training exercises.

Vitamin supplements, such as powdered vitamins and minerals, can be found at animal supply displays. They are intended to be mixed into the rat's drinking water. This can lead to bacterial growth inside the containers, which in turn can cause diarrhea or dehydration because the rat doesn't like the taste of the water and will not drink it. There is no need to add supplements of this type if you are feeding your rat a well-balanced, high-quality diet. Over-supplementation is as dangerous to your pet's health as deficiency!

Feeding Your Sick Rat

Loss of appetite is one of the first signs that your rat is not feeling well. If this lasts for more than a day, you should take the rat to your veterinarian for a thorough physical examination.

In addition to medication and other nursing care, you may have to make a special effort to feed your rat until it is feeling better.

The most important thing you can provide for your sick rat is water to prevent dehydration. Take advantage of your rat's sweet tooth to add some carbohydrates for energy. Sweeten water with a small amount of table sugar, or powdered fruit-flavored drink mix or gelatin. Your rat may drink it from a dropper or syringe once you put the first drop into its mouth. But go easy with this; too much sugar will cause gastric upset and diarrhea. Alternate plain or sweetened water with electrolyte replacement fluids such as Pedialyte.

T I P

Importance of Nutrition

Aside from hygiene, nutrition is the one factor you can control to ensure that your rat has a long and healthy life. The importance of a wholesome, well-balanced diet, free from chemicals and additives, cannot be overemphasized.

Baby food, smashed banana, or smashed avocado, diluted in soy formula (for human babies) or Esbilac (canine milk replacer) or KMR (kitten milk replacer) can be used to feed sick or rehabilitating rats, using a dropper or syringe.

Potentially Harmful Foods

Do not feed your rats cooked or processed foods. They are not good for them and may be deficient in vitamins and minerals or contain food additives and preservatives.

Do not feed your rat candies. They are fattening and high in sugar. In addition, hard candies may pose a choking risk.

Water

Water is one of the most important components of your pet's diet! The best water you can provide your rats is the same water you filter or buy for yourself. The quality of well water and city water may vary and could contain high levels of undesirable elements, such as arsenic or iron, or additives such as chlorine and chloramine.

✔ Make sure your rats have plenty of fresh drinking water available at all times. As most of your pets' diet is dry (commercial rodent blocks, pellets), the need for water is greater.

✔ Water consumption depends on your pet's health, activity level, age, and condition. If your rat is pregnant or lactating, she may drink two to three times more water than a rat that is not pregnant or nursing a litter.

✔ The higher the temperature and the lower the humidity, the more water your pet will need to drink.

You also can try baby cereal, grits, or cream of wheat. Make sure the cereal isn't too hot; room temperature or slightly above is best. It's easy to overdo it when you use a microwave oven. Applesauce and plain or flavored yogurt can also be syringe-fed.

Protein-rich foods, like cooked eggs or strained meat baby food (chicken, beef, veal, and lamb), are easily lapped by an ailing rat. A commercially prepared prescription diet, manufactured by Hill's Pet Products called a/d, is a high fat, high protein, highly palatable diet designed for nutritional support during recovery. Although it is designed for canine and feline patients, its composition and palatability make it a good choice for sick, anorexic rats. It is a pureed diet that easily can be syringe-fed if your rat is unwilling to eat it on its own. Prescription diet a/d is available through your veterinarian. Other syringable products that you can try include soy based nutritional drinks such as Ensure, or Pediasure, and a gel-like nutritional supplement called Nutrical that comes in a tube. Even though your rat may not be eating much of its regular fare right now, have some available for when it begins to eat on its own again.

HEALTH

Once you have spent some time with your rat, feeding, cleaning its habitat, playing, and perhaps doing some training, you will come to learn its unique behaviors. You will soon recognize its favorite foods, when and where it likes to sleep, its preferred places to be scratched, even its favorite places to explore while out of its enclosure.

Choosing a Veterinarian

Rats are generally hardy animals that do very well when given excellent care and a nutritious, balanced diet. However, if your rat becomes sick or is injured, you may need to take it to a veterinarian for an examination and possible treatment. The sooner your rat is diagnosed and treated, the better its chances are for a speedy recovery.

Some veterinarians specialize in very small pets and exotic, or nonconventional, pets. Very small pets, such as rats, have nutritional, housing, and medical requirements that are very different from the larger companion animals, such as dogs, cats, or horses. Small pets can be sensitive to certain products and medications used for treating more common pets. They may also require special equipment for performing surgical procedures. For these reasons, whenever possible, it is wise to choose a veterinarian who has expertise and experience in diagnosing and treating rats. If you do not know of a veterinarian in your area, you can contact the Association of Exotic Mammal Veterinarians (*www.aemv.org*, see Information) for a list of veterinarians in your area who have a special interest and expertise in rat medicine and surgery.

Signs of Illness

Behavior, appetite, haircoat, weight, body condition, and the color, consistency, and frequency of droppings and urine all reflect the general state of health of your rat. Watch for anything out of the ordinary: labored or noisy breathing, discharge from the eyes or nose, sneezing, diarrhea, diminished appetite, changes in drinking or urine, scratching or hair loss, limping, or loss of balance. In this section, you will learn about some of the rat's organs, how they show illness, and some of the diseases you may observe in your rat.

Skin

Did you know that the skin, or integument, is the largest organ system of the body? It is

the first line of defense that rats and other living creatures have against the environment and disease. The rat's skin and its adjoining structures—fur, nails, glands, whiskers, and lashes—all serve as a defense against predators and the elements.

The fur or pelt insulates the rat against the cold and precipitation. Sebaceous glands under the skin secrete oils that make the fur somewhat waterproof. Rats recognize each other through chemicals in these oils. Tiny muscles in the skin attach to the hair shaft and cause the hairs to stand up higher (piloerection). This creates a thicker barrier against the cold, like the hair on your arms when you have goose

bumps. Fur also protects against bites from the long incisor teeth of other rats and predators. The agouti banding of the hair shaft is a neutral pattern that acts as camouflage for the wild rat.

Rats do not sweat, except from glands in the leathery pads on the bottoms of their feet; they become overheated easily. Toenails are used for climbing, grooming, defense, and for grasping objects. Whiskers (vibrissae) on the face and scattered over the body are equipped with special sensory nerves that allow the rat to navigate through small spaces and along walls and crevices. Eyelashes sweep away debris to protect the surface of the eye.

Skin, fur, nails, whiskers, and lashes are all affected by nutrition, infection, trauma, aging, parasites, and chemicals in the environment. And there are only a limited number of ways that the skin can respond to these influences. With the help of some simple diagnostic tests, a veterinarian can find the answers to most common skin problems in rats. Symptoms of diseases related to the skin include:

✔ hair loss
✔ scratching
✔ rubbing
✔ chewing
✔ swelling
✔ redness
✔ scaling
✔ sores

Ears, Eyes, Nose, and Lungs

The ears, eyes, and nose are sense organs. Besides providing the sense of hearing, the ears play an important role in the sense of balance, too, which is extremely well developed in the rat. The nose provides the sense of smell and filters dust, germs, pollen, and other debris from the air before it enters the lungs. Air passing through the nose is also warmed and humidified to protect delicate lung tissue from damaging dryness.

Diseases of the eyes and upper respiratory system are some of the most important diseases of rats. Persistent tilting of the head, swaggered gait, reddish brown staining around the eyes or nose, face rubbing, and sneezing are all signs of diseases that involve the upper respiratory tract, eyes, and ears in rats. Wheezing, labored breathing, poor appetite, weight loss, hunched posture, chattering, and lethargy suggest problems involving the lungs.

The Heart and Circulation

The heart is a unique muscle. One of the heart's functions is to receive oxygen-depleted blood from the tissues and to pump it out into the lungs to be replenished with oxygen. Another of the heart's functions is to pump the restored blood returning from the lungs back out into the body. This is accomplished within a system of channels called arteries and veins. Like the rest of the body, these organs are subject to the effects of aging and stress. Aside from their general deterioration as an animal gets older, there are no specific diseases of the heart and circulation important to the pet rat.

Abdominal Organs

A mammal's body is divided into two cavities by a muscular structure called the diaphragm. The thorax lies in front of the diaphragm and contains the heart and lungs. The abdomen, behind the diaphragm, contains the liver, stomach, intestines, kidneys, bladder, reproductive organs, and some important glands. Bodily processes vital to the digestion of food, assimilation of nutrients, excretion of wastes, conservation of water, and reproduction take place in the abdomen. Diseases in these organs cause:

✔ diarrhea
✔ weight loss
✔ poor appetite
✔ bloating
✔ discharges vaginal
✔ infertility
✔ lethargy
✔ excessive water consumption and urination

Muscles and Bones

Bones, muscles, tendons, and ligaments connect together to form a skeleton that protects the internal organs and allows for locomotion. But did you know that there are bones in the ear and muscles in the intestines? Limping, holding up a paw, and abnormal angles to limbs indicate diseases of bones and muscles. These diseases are usually the result of some trauma, or growth or genetic defect. They are potentially painful problems; your rat may try to bite you if you examine it. Minor muscle soreness, sprains, and strains usually disappear in a day or two if the rat rests. Your veterinarian should investigate persistent lameness.

Nervous System

Nerve tissues carry chemical impulses throughout the body, directing all the other organs in their physiologic functions. This is somewhat analogous to electrical lines carrying power to homes and businesses, with the brain and spinal cord as the power plant. Nerve tissue is subject to the same effects of nutrition, chemicals, aging, and trauma as all other tissues in the body. In rats, aging and trauma have the greatest effect on the nervous system. Diseases of the nervous system manifest themselves in the rat as:

✔ incoordination
✔ trembling
✔ seizures
✔ paralysis
✔ depression

Miscellaneous Diseases

Because they are used in medical research, there is a great body of knowledge about diseases of rats. And there are lots of strains of rats (and mice) that have developed diseases and conditions similar to ones in humans that have then been bred specifically for research in these areas. This is accomplished mostly through carefully controlled line breeding of genetically mutated animals. Because genetic mutations occur spontaneously within every species, there are unexpected and unexplainable diseases appearing in the pet rat population, too. With all this in mind, this section is limited to the diseases and conditions that concern most rat fanciers.

Abscesses

An abscess is an accumulation of bacteria and pus cells under the skin creating a warm, soft, and sometimes painful swelling. The skin over an abscess becomes red and purplish, and the hair over an abscess can be plucked out at the roots quite easily, leaving a bald patch. Abscesses are caused by germs introduced through a puncture or bite wound, or through the bloodstream. Abscesses also occur without an injury in old, debilitated, and malnourished animals. When the pressure from the fluid is great enough, an abscess ruptures through the surface of the skin and drains a milky, foul-smelling discharge, gray-ish green to yellow in color. Left untreated, an abscess may continue to fester, or the infection can spread to other parts of the body. If you sus-pect that your rat has an abscess, call your vet-erinarian. Some abscesses are actually infected tumors. Abscesses are treated with antibiotics, warm compresses, and sometimes surgery.

Tumors

Tumors, both benign and malignant, are very common in rats. They can appear even at a young age.

Benign tumors do not spread to other organs, but they may interfere by taking up space, pushing normal tissues out of the way, or by leaving a rat unable to walk. If not surgi-cally removed, they often outgrow their blood supply, resulting in gangrene of the tumor itself. When this happens, toxic substances from the dying tumor are absorbed into the body, and the animal can become sick or die.

Malignant tumors spread to other parts of the body, very often the lungs. This can cause difficulty breathing, loss of appetite, weight loss, lethargy, and eventually, death. Your veterinarian should examine any swelling or deformity. Small malignant tumors sometimes can be removed before they have a chance to spread.

Mammary tumors are the most common tumors seen in rats. Mammary tissue is located under the skin from the axilla or armpits, all the way along the chest and abdomen, to the inguinal area or inner thighs. Any mass or swelling in these areas could be a mammary tumor even if there is no adjacent nipple.

About 90 percent of all mammary tumors are benign. However, they can become huge and gangrenous and infected. Ten percent or so of all mammary tumors are malignant, spreading mostly to the lymph nodes and lungs, although they can spread to bone and other organs. Benign and malignant mammary tumors look the same; only a biopsy can tell them apart. Because mammary tumors often become large and cumbersome, they should be removed, even if benign, and preferably when small.

There is strong evidence to suggest that ovariohysterectomy or "spaying" female rats can nearly eliminate the incidence of mam-mary tumors as it does in other animals, like

Creating an Incubator

An incubator environment where the temperature is a few degrees higher can benefit many seriously ill and anorexic animals that have trouble keeping warm. This is easily accomplished in several ways. These patients should be isolated in small cages or aquaria away from other rats. To raise the temperature, place a heating pad under the habitat. Set the pad's thermostat on low and put a towel between the pad and the cage or aquarium to prevent the temperature inside from becoming too high. If you are isolating your rat in a cage, place another towel over most of the cage to retain the heat. You can also fasten a heating pad to the side of a cage with clothespins and then cover the cage with a towel.

Other objects that can be placed inside the habitat to warm it are empty soda bottles filled with warm water, traditional hot water bottles, and a reusable, microwavable, disk-shaped device called a Snuggle Safe, from Thermal Concepts LTD. Place a thermometer inside the incubator and monitor the temperature closely. Rats are very sensitive to high temperatures. The temperature inside

the incubator should not exceed 80°F and the humidity should not drop below 40 percent at any time (55 percent is preferable).

If you have several rats, or if you are involved in a rat club, rat rescue, or rat rehabilitation, consider purchasing a commercial incubator designed specifically for small animals. An excellent product is the ThermoCare Animal Intensive Care Unit (*www.thermocare.com*). It is a water-controlled incubator (eliminating the risk of burns as commonly occurs when using a heating pad) and is also a humidifier.

Never use heat lamps to warm you rat. They are drying and can cause burns and overheating. If you use a heating pad under the incubator, it is safest to use a water heating pad, rather than an electric heating pad. Electric heating pads can cause thermal burns and overheating.

Watch your rat for panting and overheating. If you put the heating pad under the cage, put it under only half of it so that your rat can move off the heat if it wishes. Never place an immobile rat on top of a heating pad as thermal burns can result.

dogs and cats. You can consider spaying your rats to prevent mammary tumors if there is a veterinary surgeon with experience in abdominal surgery in rats in your area. Both spaying and surgical removal of tumors require general anesthesia. Spaying is more invasive and risky a surgery than removing most small to moderately sized mammary tumors. However, while spaying is generally done on young

animals, mammary tumors usually occur in middle-aged to older rats, making anesthesia a little trickier. You should discuss these issues with your veterinarian.

External Parasites

Most scaling, scabbing, itching, and hair loss in rats is due to an infestation of fur mites or lice, and occasionally fleas. Flea control is rather straightforward these days, however fur mites and lice can be two of the most insidious and frustrating problems to correct, especially for rat fanciers who keep large numbers of rats. All three parasites are highly contagious and can live on healthy animals and cause no apparent disease. These animals are called "asymptomatic carriers" in the vernacular of the epidemiologist.

When infested animals are introduced into a colony, pet store population, or home, these parasites quickly spread to other animals through direct contact or by inanimate objects like towels, bedding, toys, and so on that are contaminated with the parasites' eggs. Once a population of rats is infested, *all the animals*—not just the ones with skin problems—must be treated with an appropriate course of medication, and the environment must be carefully cleaned to remove eggs.

Cleaning up the environment poses the biggest problem for people who allow their rats to roam in the house. All newly acquired rats should be quarantined for a minimum of three weeks before being introduced to the others. New rats should be examined carefully for fleas, mites, and lice and you should consider having all new rats treated for mites and lice *even if an infestation is not discovered.*

Mange: Mites inhabit the skin and hair follicles in all creatures. Most species of mites are commensal animals, living in the skin in small numbers, causing no harm to the host. In sick, debilitated, malnourished, or old animals, mites flourish because the immune system in these animals is unable to keep their numbers in check. This condition is called mange.

Mites burrow through the skin, eating skin cells and inciting an inflammation that can cause hair loss, greasiness, scaling, redness, and severe itching. Rats will scratch, creating sores on their skin, especially in the areas behind the ears and along the back. Your veterinarian can diagnose mange by scraping the rat's skin with a small metal spatula or scalpel blade, putting the flakes of skin onto a clean glass slide along with a drop of oil, and looking for mites or mite eggs in the specimen with a microscope.

Fur mites can be controlled with medication that is given orally, topically, or by injection. A spot-on drug called selemectin is also used. The itching can remain intense even after treatment because the dead mites in the skin continue to cause inflammation. Medicated shampoos will help with itch relief and the sores. Antibiotics are not usually necessary.

It's unlikely that you will completely eliminate the infestation, although you should be able to eliminate the dermatitis. You should pay special attention to nutrition, other underlying diseases, and husbandry. Fur mites do not live long off an animal, and they don't infest humans or other pets. You should clean the rat's habitat thoroughly to eliminate mite eggs.

Fleas: Typically we think of these tiny jumpers as being pests to dogs and cats, but unlike the other skin parasites of rats, fleas will infest most mammals. Only adult fleas live on animals where they feed, mate, and lay eggs. The eggs are not sticky, but fall freely off the animal and into the environment: your home. There they hatch free-living larvae that eat skin scales and other organic debris. Larvae form pupae just like butterfly caterpillars do. Adult fleas emerge from the pupae and immediately must find a host, or they will die. They don't see very well so they simply fling themselves on any warm body that happens by: your dog, your cat, your free-ranging rat, or you. Naturally, one animal can infest another through close contact. In a low-level infestation, you may not see the adult fleas on your rat, but rather their droppings. These droppings are little black flecks of dried blood in the fur or on bedding that dissolve into a reddish brown liquid when they get wet.

These days it is entirely possible to completely eliminate a flea infestation from pets and the home, often without using environmental treatments. The key to eliminating fleas from your rats is to eliminate them from other household pets by using any one of a number of oral or topical products available through your veterinarian or other pet health suppliers. These products work not only by killing and repelling fleas, but also by breaking the flea life cycle. You can kill the fleas on your rats by bathing them in a diluted pyrethrin-based flea shampoo safe for use on cats. Regular shampoos don't repel fleas. If your rat still gets fleas despite treating the household dogs and cats, you will need to use products that eliminate the environmental infestation, and probably a topical product like a pyrethrin powder or spray, or selemectin. Contact your veterinarian for assistance in getting rid of these nuisances.

Lice: Lice are one of the most difficult skin parasites to eliminate because many rats are asymptomatic carriers. Lice are tiny, translucent, flat creatures that hold on to the hair shaft of the host. They produce eggs called "nits" that they "glue" to hair. When the eggs hatch, the infestation intensifies. Lice are spread by direct contact of one infested animal to another. They also are spread when hairs and eggs are shed into the environment and are contacted by other animals.

━━━━━ T I P ━━━━━

Lowdown on Lice

Lice are species-specific: that is, they live on only one host. Rats cannot give humans lice, and humans cannot transmit lice to rats!

They cause intense itching and direct damage to the skin. Damage also results from the rat's furious scratching.

Lice infestation is common in pet stores where there are lots of rats, frequent introduction of new rats probably from more than one source, and a lack of quarantine for new animals. Because lice are highly contagious, sanitation and husbandry don't have to be bad, but they often are, at least at the animals' source. Infestation often goes unnoticed in young and healthy animals whose immune systems can keep the pests in check. Older rats and those weakened by disease, transport, and reproduction are the ones most likely to be noticed and treated, leaving the asymptomatic carriers to maintain the infestation within an ever shifting population. Someone comes in and buys an apparently healthy rat and puts it in with their existing rat pets and *poof*—that colony is infested too!

The lice themselves are easily killed using a pyrethrin-based shampoo and flea powder, but the eggs, or "nits," are difficult to dislodge from the hair shaft. For that reason, infested rats must be retreated every 7 to 10 days until all the nits or eggs have hatched and the lice have been killed. Hairs contaminated with eggs

must be removed from the environment to prevent reinfestation. That means the habitat must be cleaned frequently and if your rats play loose in your house, the house must be cleaned and vacuumed to remove rodent hairs, too. Lice can be treated systemically with ivermectin and selemectin, too.

All newly acquired rats should be quarantined for at least three weeks before being introduced into a colony. It's a good idea to prophylactically treat new rats for lice unless you are certain that they come from a lice-free breeder or pet store that is meticulous about husbandry and sanitation.

Foot and Nail Injuries

Rats housed in wire mesh cages are susceptible to foot and nail injuries. The pressure and irritation of the wire cause calluses to form on the feet that can swell and become infected. Toes and nails can catch in crevices and break

or tear. Toes and feet sustain injury during rough play sessions between cage mates, too. If towels are used for bedding material, threads can wrap around the feet and cut off the circulation. And of course, when outside the cage, rats are susceptible to all sorts of potential foot and nail trauma from being stepped on, dropped, trapped, or caught.

Remarkably, most foot injuries don't become infected, but torn nails do tend to bleed or spot. Infection is a problem when wounds are contaminated with dirty bedding and feces from poor husbandry. Injury, especially circulation injuries, and infections cause lameness and even loss of toes or the entire foot.

In case of injury with bleeding, apply pressure to the area with a clean cloth until the bleeding stops. You can apply ice briefly to help this. Torn nails usually regrow within a few weeks. Wash sores on the feet with mild soap and rinse with water once or twice a day.

Keep the bedding material clean. Change the floor surface in the habitat to one that offers more solid footing. Plexiglas and plastic mesh canvas, available through craft supply stores, are good products for this purpose. Watch injured toes and feet for redness, pain, swelling, or discharge. These signs suggest infection and antibiotics may be needed.

Conjunctivitis and Keratitis

Conjunctivitis is defined as an inflammation of the tissues surrounding the eye. Conjunctivitis causes tearing and discharge, swelling around the neck, red and swollen eyelids, hair loss, reddish-brown staining around the eyes and nose, face-rubbing, and sneezing. If conjunctivitis is severe, it may involve the eye itself, causing the cornea to turn cloudy or bluish, and to ulcerate. Inflammation of the cornea is called *keratitis*. Conjunctivitis and keratitis are almost always caused by viral and bacterial infections. These problems are often complicated by high ammonia concentrations inside cages, dust and chemicals in bedding, or detergent and disinfectant residues. Conjunctivitis and keratitis can also result from trauma.

You may think the reddish-brown staining is blood, but it is not. Tear glands located behind the eyes produce their secretions in excess during periods of illness and stress. These secretions contain substances called porphyrins. Porphyrin staining around the face is not a specific sign of conjunctivitis; rather it is a general sign of illness, nutritional deficiency, husbandry problems, and aging.

Sialodacryoadentitis Virus (SDA) is the most well-recognized viral cause of conjunctivitis in rats. It can infect any age rat, but once a rat has had the infection and recovered, it cannot acquire the infection again. SDA virus infects the saliva and tear-producing glands around the face and eyes. Rats become infected through contact with each other and with objects contaminated with secretions. You can introduce it into your rat population by bringing home an infected rat and plunking it in with the others without quarantine. You can also introduce it by handling infected rats at, say a pet store or a rat show, and then handling your own without washing your hands. Some strains of rats are more susceptible to conjunctivitis caused by SDA virus than others and there is no way to know if your rats are or not.

The biggest problem with SDA virus conjunctivitis is that it often results in secondary infection by more serious germs like mycoplasma. When this happens, simple conjunctivitis can turn into a debilitating or even life-threatening

disease. SDA virus infection is a self-limiting disease. That means if you don't introduce any more rats into your household (that includes no breeding), all the animals eventually will get SDA virus, become immune, and the virus will go away. This will take about two months. You must carefully review your sanitation and husbandry practices. Are you cleaning your cages often enough and properly? Do you quarantine new animals?

Treatments for conjunctivitis and keratitis include ointments and systemic antibiotics. Eliminating environmental stressors, like reducing ammonia levels inside the habitat, eliminating household smoking, introduction of new rats, proper bedding and nutrition, helps with therapy. Conjunctivitis is often a recurrent problem if the cause is infectious in nature and the environmental factors are ignored.

Upper Respiratory Infections and Pneumonia

This is probably the most common health problem in rats. Sneezing, porphyrin staining around the eyes and nose, wheezing, hunched posture, chattering, ruffled and unkempt haircoat, and labored breathing are all signs of upper respiratory infections. Virtually all rats are infected early in life with a number of bacteria and viruses responsible for respiratory diseases. These germs live in harmony with the animal in the respiratory passages until certain conditions exist, such as infection, poor hygiene or nutrition, injury, or lowered resistance to disease simply due to aging. For this reason, most rats show signs of respiratory disease by the time they reach one year of age.

Pneumonia is a severe and frequent consequence of upper respiratory infections espe-

cially in older rats. Progressive damage to the airways and lung tissues results in severely labored breathing, dehydration, starvation, and eventual death. Recovery from pneumonia is sometimes possible with demanding supportive care: intensive nursing, strong antibiotics, medications to open up airways, and hand feeding.

Mycoplasma pulmonis is the most important respiratory disease-causing pathogen in rats. You can assume that all rats are infected with this bacteria; it can be considered an opportunistic commensal. Rats become infected through contact with each other and through inanimate objects like water bottles or your clothing. Rats can acquire their infection before they are born as pregnant rats pass mycoplasma to their offspring in the uterus. Mycoplasma is impossible to eliminate from a colony of pet rats. Researchers using rats can do so only with an extensive testing program, isolation procedures, and Cesarian-derived offspring!

Most mycoplasmal infections are silent and do not cause anything other than low-grade signs of upper respiratory disease. Signs often tend to wax and wane; animals that are treated with antibiotics seem to get better and in many cases, the signs would have waned on their own. In chronic infections, rats may need lifelong antibiotics.

Mycoplasma can cause pneumonia and even infertility. Severe disease usually results when rats are also infected with other pathogens, like SDA virus, that come in and do the initial damage to the respiratory tract, allowing mycoplasma and other bacteria (or viruses) to take over and make things worse. Some strains of mycoplasma that are more virulent or damaging than others. All rats are not equally susceptible to mycoplasma; some are more resistant than others. And of course, you have to consider environmental factors too, like hygiene, ammonia levels inside the habitat, dust, and smoke that are simply damaging and toxic to the airways and lungs on their own.

If all this seems rather bleak and hopeless, don't despair. There are lots of breeders out there who are trying to minimize mycoplasma as a disease agent in the pet rat population by breeding resistant rats, and eliminating the more pathogenic strains of the bacteria from the breeding population. This is one of the most compelling arguments for breed registries and for acquiring your rats from reputable breeders.

Other infectious agents cause upper respiratory infections and pneumonia in rats, sometimes alone but usually in concert with others. *Sendai virus, Pasteurella, cilia-associated respiratory bacillus,* and *Haemophilus* are just a few that you may come across in other sources. The type of treatment that you may choose (or not choose) should depend on probability of infection, likely pathogen, the rat's age and other underlying diseases, environmental factors, and availability. Avoid indiscriminate use of antibiotics. This leads to drug resistance.

Kidney Disease

The kidneys are responsible for many complex functions in the body. Some of their main functions are to remove waste products from blood and to conserve water. As in other animals, as rats age, their kidneys slowly lose the ability to perform these functions. Rats and other animals compensate for this to some degree by drinking more water in an effort to flush out waste products through the remaining healthy kidney tissue. As a consequence, more urine is produced. This change in water consumption and urination may be difficult to notice in rats. Eventually, there is not enough healthy kidney tissue left to meet the body's requirement, and kidney failure occurs.

Aside from changes in thirst and urination, you may notice other things like weight loss or worsening of upper respiratory infections. Your veterinarian can take a blood sample and test it for urea, one of the waste products that typically rises in the blood when the kidneys are failing and have lost at least 75 percent of their function.

Kidney disease is not curable. It is slowly progressive in all animals. You can support the remaining healthy kidney tissue and make your rat feel better with fluids and diet. The possibility that diets high in protein hasten the development of kidney disease has been a hot topic in medicine for decades. The controversy is over whether dietary protein should be reduced in animals as they age, how much and at what age and species, and whether it affects the progressive deterioration of the kidneys. The majority of scientists believe that while reducing protein levels doesn't slow down the kidney disease, it may make the animals feel better because it reduces the kidney's workload. The kidneys have less urea (one of the waste products of dietary protein) to remove. Lower blood urea means less depression, less thirst, and better quality of life.

Much of the research has been done on experimental models of renal failure in rats and dogs, not on the natural disease, so people argue over the validity of the conclusions that are drawn from the results. It is extremely important not to automatically assume that

diseases behave the same in all species of animals. However, if lower dietary protein levels make other animals like dogs and cats with renal disease feel better, it makes sense that restricting dietary protein in aging rats may make them feel better, too. And you may be slowing the disease process as well. Your veterinarian can advise you on how to use fluids and diet to manage your aging rat.

Megacolon

This is a condition seen in very young rats, usually only a few weeks old. Affected rats are sluggish and do not eat well. They develop a distended abdomen from constipation and then paradoxically, diarrhea. These animals are underweight and thin from malnutrition, and eventually die despite efforts to force-feed them. The disease resembles Hirschsprung's Disease in children and results when the nerves that supply the colon do not develop, or the chemicals necessary for these nerves to function are not present. Necropsies on these rats show segments of narrowed bowel and segments of very distended bowel. Affected children are treated with surgery. This is an inherited disease in humans and rats. Because megacolon is always fatal in affected rats, the best we can do is to prevent the trait from being passed from non-affected gene carrying rats to their offspring. The parents of rats with megacolon should not be used for breeding.

Degenerative Myelopathy

Aging rats, most frequently those older than two years of age, may become uncoordinated or paralyzed in the rear legs due to a degenerative process of the nerves that carry impulses to the muscles of the limbs. It is not a fatal disease; however, it can be very debilitating in its

later stages. The animal may be unable to move around the cage well, and eventually may not be able to reach food or water. Outside its habitat, the rat is at greater risk of injury from falls and aggression from other animals. Calluses and sores develop on the knees from crawling and these may become infected.

Ringtail

If relative humidity is consistently less than 40 percent in its environment, young rats may develop annular or ring-like sores and scars around the tail on one or more locations. In severe cases, the end of the tail may fall off, leaving a stump. This condition is commonly found in one- to two-week-old domestic rats born during the winter months, when indoor air is usually very dry. It is also more common in rats housed in cages or when processed corncob, which is dehydrating, is used for bedding. To prevent subsequent litters of babies from being affected, raise the relative humidity by changing to an aquarium habitat. A room or furnace humidifier also helps. If you are using processed corncob for bedding, change to aspen shavings or a paper product.

Overgrown Teeth

The rat's four front teeth, or incisors, grow continuously—at a rate of about 4 to 5 inches

(10.5 to 13 cm) a year. They require constant grinding through the rat's natural gnawing behavior to keep them at a functional length. If the upper and lower incisors are not aligned with one another, normal wear cannot take place and the teeth eventually will curve to the side or penetrate the cheek. This condition, called a malocclusion, occurs if either the upper or lower jaw is too short or too long, or if there has been some trauma to the face that knocks the incisors out of alignment. Dental problems with the molar teeth are also possible, but this is less common. Rats with a malocclusion should not be used for breeding because this harmful trait is passed to the offspring.

Overgrown teeth must be trimmed periodically to allow the rat to eat and to prevent sores and infection in the mouth. This can be done using a nail trimmer or side cutting wire cutters in cooperative rats.

Wrap your rat in a hand towel, leaving the animal's head exposed. Using a folding nail trimmer or side-cutting wire cutting tool, snip the curved overgrown section of the upper and lower incisors to the length of approximately ½ inch (1 cm). Trimming one tooth at a time may help to prevent splitting.

If the teeth are very overgrown and penetrating tissue, your veterinarian should do the procedure under general anesthesia so that the mouth can be thoroughly examined. This holds true for large rats, ones with severe infections, and uncooperative rats as well. Antibiotics will be necessary to treat any infection.

Overgrown Nails

Long nails should be trimmed to prevent them from catching and being torn. Examine your rat's nails for the pink center, or "quick," containing sensitive tissue and capillaries. The quick will bleed if you cut the nail too short. Use a folding trimmer to remove just the sharp tips of the nails. If bleeding occurs, apply pressure to the end of the nail. Then quickly release the pressure and apply a pinch of silver nitrate (Kwik Stop) powder, flour, or cornstarch to the momentarily dry tip to stop the bleeding.

Skin Infections and Parasites

Medicated baths are used to treat skin infections and external parasites like mites and lice. Pyrethrin-based shampoos, products containing surgical scrubs, and others labeled for use on cats are generally safe for rats. To avoid irritating the rat's eyes with soap and water, you can instill a small amount of bland ointment before you start. Follow the instructions on the bottle for length of application; most require a five to ten minute contact time before rinsing with plenty of clear warm water. Then towel dry thoroughly.

Zoonoses

Earlier, we talked about diseases wild rats transmit to humans through direct contact and through contamination of food and water with droppings and urine. Diseases that animals transmit to people are called *zoonoses*. Zoonotic diseases of wild rats do not occur in laboratory or commercially bred rats.

The most common problems researchers and rat fanciers encounter are allergic reactions to urine, proteins in rat, dander, saliva, and hair, and injury or infection secondary to rat bites. The incidence of these problems is unknown, because they are not required by law to be reported to disease control centers. If you have respiratory problems, you should discuss how your rats might affect these conditions with your physician.

While most of the organisms harbored by pet rats are not a problem for people, rats are known to carry organisms such as *Leptospira, Salmonella,* and *Pneumocystis carnii* with significant frequency. These organisms pose little or no threat to healthy people, but they *can* pose a threat to people whose immune systems are not working well, such as those who are immunosuppressed (such as by chemotherapy).

Risks of Anesthesia and Surgery

There is no such thing as 100 percent risk-free surgery, in any species. Some of the risks or complications include death, excessive bleeding, respiratory or cardiac arrest, hypothermia, infection, and failure of the surgical wound to heal because the animal or its housemate licks or picks at it, or removes the sutures. It's important to realize that these risks exist regardless of the surgeon's skill or the animal's underlying health problems. What can vary with those factors is the *degree* of risk.

Careful patient selection is very important. A rat burdened with a large mammary tumor but a healthy pair of lungs is a much better candidate for surgery than one also suffering from chronic or recurrent pneumonia. Careful patient monitoring during the procedure can reduce the risk of respiratory and cardiac arrest. An external source of heat, like a warm water bottle, can reduce the risk of hypothermia during and after a procedure.

Obviously, the surgeon's skill is critical. Even with all possible precautions in place, some problems, including fatalities, do occur because, when working with biological systems, all factors cannot be known and controlled.

These individuals should make their physician aware of all household pets including rats.

The Geriatric Rat

By 18 months, rats of both sexes begin to develop changes in their internal organs, muscles, nerves, and bones related to old age. By the time it is two years old, a rat is considered old. Despite the changes occurring inside their bodies, many pet rats can live to the age of three, four, or even five years, although that is rare.

Rats have been used for decades in research on nutrition, cancer, heart disease, obesity, learning, toxicology, aging, and just about every other branch of biological science. Because of this research, much is known about aging in rats—what goes on at the level of the cell, the organ, and ultimately the whole body. A rat's aging depends on many complex interactions among genetics, nutrition, reproduction, and environmental conditions. No single factor determines whether your rat lives a long time. Attention to all these factors will optimize the chances of having a healthy, happy pet.

As your rat gets older, you may begin to notice changes in its behavior and overall body condition related to the aging process. The most common diseases of geriatric rats include tumors or cancer, chronic respiratory disease (especially pneumonia), kidney disease, and nerve deterioration. These conditions are usually accompanied by changes in water and food consumption, difficulty in breathing and walking, lethargy, and loss of weight. The signs of aging in rats do not appear suddenly overnight, but come on gradually and often without immediate notice. The rat's body has a remarkable capacity to adapt. So despite the presence of a swelling under its foreleg or a discharge from its nostrils, your rat's quality of life may be good.

Unlike humans and even other companion animals like dogs and cats, there is not a lot

that can be done to cure some of the diseases in older rats. Diabetic dogs can be given insulin injections; kidney disease can be controlled with fluid therapy and medication. These measures are impractical if not impossible to do to a 10½ ounce (300 gm) rat. However, many tumors can be removed, especially if they are small. This may not lengthen the life of your rat, but it may improve the quality of its life. Your veterinarian can help you decide if a surgical procedure is appropriate.

Euthanasia
Most people want to avoid taking any active part in the death of an animal, especially making the decision to end a life even for humane reasons. Your veterinarian can help you with this decision; not every circumstance is the same.

The same basic principles of first aid that are used on larger companion animals and humans also apply to the nursing of sick and injured rodents. If your rat has fallen, become trapped by a door or a drawer, been stepped on, bitten by the dog, or scratched by the cat, return it to its own habitat or isolate it in a smaller one if there are several other rats, and watch it carefully. Apply direct pressure to any bleeding wounds using a clean cloth or gauze and your fingers, but otherwise your pet should be left alone to recover from the trauma. If bleeding, lameness, breathing difficulty, depression, or pain persists, your rat may have a fracture or internal injury, so call your veterinarian. Don't try to apply a bandage or splint yourself. You may apply one improperly and cut off the circulation to the limb.

Administering Medicine

During the course of treatment for any illness or injury, your veterinarian may prescribe medication to be administered into the rat's eyes or mouth, or into the drinking water. You may be instructed to clean and treat wounds, give medicated baths, watch surgical wounds for infection, or other special treatments. Make sure that you fully understand the veterinarian's instructions, and don't hesitate to ask for a demonstration or tips on restraining your rat for these procedures. Many are described here.

Many of the common antibiotics used on rodents are palatable to rats, so oral medications usually are not a problem for owners who have rats that are used to being handled. However, ointments and a few of the procedures can be frightening or uncomfortable for the rat, and it may struggle. You can safely immobilize a rat by scruffing it or by rolling the rat in a small towel and leaving its head exposed. These techniques are described in Rat Restraint, page 41.

Liquid medicine is usually given by mouth and is dispensed by the veterinarian in a bottle or sometimes a rubber stoppered glass tube, and administered with a medicine dropper or small syringe. Some oral medications are clear solutions, others are thick, flavored suspensions that are prepared by adding water to a powdered drug. Most veterinary offices will prepare these suspensions for you, but they require thorough shaking before you draw up the appropriate dose. Refrigeration may be recommended. Warm and prepare the appropriate dose before you have your rat in your hand so that you don't fumble and spill it. If you hold a drop at your rat's lips, it will probably lick it. If not, insert the end of the dropper or

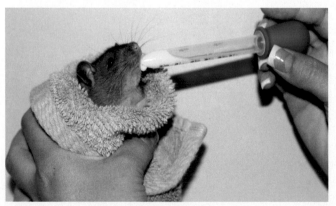

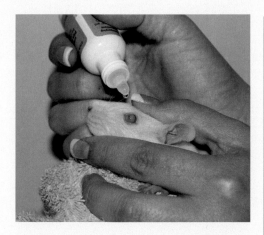

syringe into the diastema and squirt the medicine into its mouth.

Some medications simply taste nasty to your rat and you will need to disguise their flavor. Rats love sweets so flavoring the medication with juice, honey, syrup, or powdered fruit drink mix or gelatin may do the trick. Don't dilute the medication with any more flavoring than you can successfully administer by syringe or dropper or you will give an incorrect dose. You can also try mixing the medication into jam or applesauce or any pureed, preferably syringable, fruit or vegetable that your rat may love.

Putting medicine into drinking water ordinarily is not the best way to administer medication to sick animals, rats or otherwise. Often, the medicine doesn't taste good to the rat, so the rat may decrease the amount of water it usually drinks or refuse to drink at all. That means that your patient doesn't take its medicine or won't receive an adequate dose. Inadequate water intake also means the rat might become dehydrated and get even sicker than before.

On the other hand, if you have to medicate a lot of rats at one time for a chronic infection like an upper-respiratory disease, putting medication in the water may be the most efficient course. Medicated water should be prepared fresh every day. If you are given capsules, open the capsules and dissolve the contents in the exact amount of water according to your veterinarian's instructions. Tablets can be crushed to a fine powder between two spoons, or with a pill crusher available at any pharmacy. Be sure to ask your veterinarian if the solution remains stable when exposed to light. If not, wrap the bottle tightly in aluminum foil. Change the solution daily!

If you can't get the powder to dissolve or if flakes reappear after the bottle sits undisturbed for a while, contact your veterinarian. This could mean that there is bacterial growth inside the bottle or that a chemical reaction is occurring due to some other factors in the water. The rats may be more likely to drink medicated water if you sweeten it with a little sugar, honey, syrup, or fruit-flavored powdered drink mix. The medicated water should be your rat's only source of water during treatments. Again, *be sure your rats are actually drinking the water* so that they don't become dehydrated.

Eyedrops and ointments usually require a little more physical restraint. With your rat wrapped safely in a towel, squeeze a small amount of ointment across the affected eye. For eyedrops, hold the eyelids open with your thumb and first finger and drop in the medication without touching the tip of the bottle to anything. Gently open and shut the lids to distribute ointments across the cornea.

REPRODUCTION

Wherever you decide to obtain your rat, you may be faced with the dilemma of choosing between two or more rats that are appealing in pelt and personality. If your circumstances allow you to have more than one pair of animals, by all means, go ahead. Should you choose animals of both sexes, you may soon find yourself well stocked with rats.

Initial Considerations

Instinctively, rats are polygamous; that is, they breed with more than one other rat during their lifetime. In artificial settings, such as laboratories and breeding colonies, several breeding schemes are used to produce offspring with desired genetic traits. Rats may be inbred, which produces traits useful for specific experimental purposes. Or they may be outbred, which produces stock with variable and unpredictable characteristics.

Allowing closely related animals to mate produces inbred rat colonies. Rats mature quickly, are capable of reproducing at an early age, and have short pregnancies. This can quickly result in fairly predictable physical and physiological characteristics in the majority, if not all, the offspring. This predictability is very important for some scientific experiments. Inbreeding also allows for the development of

coat patterns and personalities pleasing to the rat fancier. This, in fact, may be your motivation in breeding rats.

Unfortunately, highly inbred animals—whether they are rats, cats, or livestock—may lack the quality of *hybrid vigor* common in animals that are more genetically varied. That is, they lack the stamina, longevity, resistance to disease, and physiologic adaptability that allows a species to thrive. So, along with the more desirable traits that breeders of animals strive to achieve, inbred rats may exhibit a greater susceptibility to cancers and infectious diseases and have shorter life spans.

That's why it is to the rat's advantage that it is polygamous. Unless you are planning to breed for a type of coat color or texture, you should not allow closely related rats in your colony to reproduce. This will maintain vigor in offspring. Before embarking on a breed-

ing project, be sure you make the necessary arrangements for care of the offspring and have homes lined up in advance for the babies. It is safe to assume that not all of your friends would appreciate the gift of a pet rat. Also, keep in mind that baby rats sold to pet stores are likely to be resold as food for snakes and other carnivorous reptiles.

Sexing Rats

   Determining the sex of a rat is best done through comparison with a litter or cage mate. Pick each one up and inspect the rats under the tails until you find two different configurations of anatomy. Males that have reached puberty have a prominent scrotum containing the testicles. When frightened or cold, male rats are capable of retracting the testicles into the body cavity. Below the scrotum is a distinctive genital papilla. Above the scrotum lies the anus.

Female rats do not have a scrotum, and the distance between the anus and external genitalia is shorter. The external genitalia in the female consist of a slit-like vulva and a small bump at the opening to the urethra.

Courtship

   In captivity as well as in the wild, the rat's sense of smell plays a tremendous role in reproduction. Both sexes communicate not only their presence to one another, but also their sexual receptivity or willingness to mate, through substances present in the urine and feces and on the skin. Male rats mark out territories by depositing drops of urine in areas where they roam. This marking behavior attracts females seeking to mate. It has been demonstrated that female rats prefer males they have mated with previously. Males do not exhibit this behavior.

Wild rats do not mature at the same rate as those born and raised in captivity. Wild female rats do not produce as many litters in their lifetime as their domestic and laboratory counterparts. This is likely due to environmental stress: climate, availability of food supplies, population density, disease, and predation. There is also variation in maturation and reproductive characteristics among strains of laboratory rats. The times for growth and gestation given in this book are averages compiled from several different sources. Your own breeding rats may not match up exactly.

To begin a rat colony, the novice breeder needs only a single pair of rats. Other breeding schemes call for one male to be housed with two to six females. If provided with enough space, the rats should get along with one another through the mating and gestation periods. More elaborate rotational schemes for breeding are used by research laboratories devoted to the production and maintenance of special strains of rats. These are less appropriate for the casual rat fancier.

The National Academy of Sciences has established guidelines for researchers working with rats. For instance, a single adolescent rat weighing about 3½ ounces (100 gm) needs a minimum of 23 square inches (148 cm²) of floor space. This is equivalent to a rectangle approximately 4 inches by 5 inches (10.5 cm by 13 cm), which is very tiny indeed. In reality, you should provide a much larger habitat

to give your pet an environment in which it can explore and move about comfortably.

Before placing two or more rats in the same breeding cage, give some attention to the size of the animals and the dimensions of the habitat. Housing rats in high density—that is, many animals in a small area—will dramatically influence their social behaviors: exploring, marking, feeding, gathering, fighting, and reproduction. Cramped quarters adds great stress. The rats may fail to breed. Or, they may fight among themselves, or resort to cannibalism of the litter.

Mating

Rats bred in captivity begin to develop sexually at about 60 days (two months) of age. As with other mammals, this period in their life is defined as puberty. There is considerable variation between strains of rats as to the age at which male and female rats are actually fertile. Some rats begin to bear young as early as 65 days of age. Most rats become fertile a little later—at around 100 days (three months). By this time most

rats weigh about 9 ounces to 10½ ounces (250–300 gm).

Once a female rat is capable of bearing young, she enters estrus (goes into heat) every four or five days. She is receptive to the male's advances for about 12 to 24 hours during the estrous cycle. Her mating behavior is controlled by fluctuations in sex hormone levels in her body, which in turn are influenced by environmental factors, such as overcrowding. Other physiologic factors, such as illness and nutritional status, also cause variations in the female rat's sexual response.

Unbred female rats continue to have a four to five day estrous cycle over and over again throughout the year until they are pregnant. If a female rat is receptive to the male, she will arch her back and present her hindquarters to him and allow him to mount. After copulation,

Fast Facts
✔ Pregnancy in rats lasts for 21 to 23 days.
✔ Babies nurse from their mothers for about three weeks.
✔ Puberty begins at about 50 to 60 days of age.
✔ Successful mating can occur by 100 days of age.
✔ Female rats are capable of producing young until they are about 15 months old.

a waxy, whitish plug fills her vagina for about 24 hours. It is called the copulatory plug, and you may find it in the cage after it has been dispelled.

Gestation and Birth

Rats carry their young in the uterus for 21 to 23 days. This is called the gestation period. You may leave a pregnant female in the habitat with the male or other pregnant females if you are using a harem breeding scheme until around day 16 of gestation. But then she should be moved to her own quarters. This is recommended because males sometimes cannibalize newborns, and because mothers do not nurse as well if they are left in the group.

Females build a nest out of the bedding material in which to give birth. Labor begins with the mother-to-be licking her vulva and the appearance of a clear vaginal discharge. The delivery takes about 1½ hours. Litter size generally ranges from 6 to 12 pups, and each pup weighs approximately .2 ounce (6 gm) at birth.

The pups are completely hairless, cannot see or hear, and are entirely dependent upon the mother for food and warmth. They even lack the ability to urinate and defecate on their own; the mother stimulates a pup to do so by licking its anus and genital papilla. You may be tempted to peek in and perhaps handle the newborn pups. Don't give in to this temptation, for disturbance of the nest may prompt the female to abandon or destroy the babies.

Raising the Pups

Be sure that the nesting cage is not subjected to drafts, fluctuations in temperature or humidity, or excessive sunlight. Temperature should be between 70° and 80°F (21° and 26°C) and humidity between 40 and 70 percent. Do not use heat lamps or other high-intensity heat sources, which can make the temperature inside the cage rise dramatically, causing overheating

and thermal burns. If the room in which you keep the cage is cooler than the recommended temperature and you must provide heat, use a hot water bottle or a heating pad set on low and clothespinned to the side of the cage. Partially cover the cage to retain the heat.

It is possible to foster orphaned pups onto another female who is nursing a litter close in age. In the wild, female rats frequently share the responsibility of raising the babies in a colony. Keep an eye on the foster mother to make sure she is eating and drinking and not becoming overburdened and weak. Also observe the foster babies to see that they have not been pushed out of the nest or cannibalized. A baby that is cold may be rejected, perhaps because the mother thinks it has died.

By 10 days of age, hair covers the pup's body and the ears and eyes have opened. Mothers begin to wean their babies as early as 21 days. At this age the pups weigh about 1½ ounces (45 gm) with the males slightly heavier than the females. During weaning, the young rats begin eating the rodent diet provided for the mother. Pups are completely weaned by 5 weeks of age. Some female rats will bite you if you handle them or their babies before they are weaned. This may occur with females that are otherwise docile and accustomed to handling when they aren't mothering a litter. You should approach any mother with caution and respect. After all, she is instinctively protecting her babies.

Female rats enter estrus again about 48 hours after delivery of a litter. It is possible to breed her again during this cycle. However, this puts an enormous strain on her body, since she now

not only must support her own tissues and organs, but also must produce sufficient milk for her babies while gestating another litter. If you wish to breed a female again, wait several weeks after weaning so her body has the opportunity to regain its strength.

Pregnant and nursing rats need the same type of nutrients that other females need: carbohydrates, proteins, fats, vitamins, and minerals. However, they need two or three times more of these nutrients, so they must eat more food. They also need more water while they are producing milk. Be sure to provide pregnant and nursing rats a fresh, well-balanced rodent diet at all times.

Under conditions of optimum husbandry, a female rat can produce a litter of offspring every month. Thankfully, this is not a realistic occurrence for rats in the wild, where variations in food supply, adequate shelter, and climate limit reproductive potential. Rat control officials tell us that a typical wild female gives birth to between three and seven litters every year.

Rats are most fertile between 3 and 10 months of age, after which the chances of conception at breeding and the number of pups per litter begin to decline. Eventually, the female's ovaries fail to produce ova or eggs and the hormones that bring on estrus. This stage in the life cycle begins at about 15 months.

Infertility

From the moment of conception, when the rat egg and sperm fuse and develop into an embryo, through to birth, many internal and external forces can cause the process to go awry. Infertility, miscarriages, resorption of

embryos, failure of young to thrive, stillbirths, or birth defects can result. Aging, disease, inadequate nutrition, overcrowding, accidents, medications, and chemical exposure are examples of these forces. Breeding closely related animals could also cause problems. Some of these forces affect the developing embryo directly. Others cause mutations, which are changes in the genes themselves.

When male and female rats are put together, offspring should soon follow. If this doesn't happen, first check to make sure you have a male and a female. Determining the sex of rats can be difficult when they're young, and mistakes are made even at pet stores. If this is not the problem, consider the age of your animals. Are they too young or too old? Also consider the habitat. Is there enough space for the animals to mate spontaneously?

Keep written records of when a male and female are put together and, if possible, of when they breed, so that the approximate delivery time can be calculated. If you have observed breeding behavior between your rats, but no pups have been delivered, the fetuses may be being resorbed during development. Be sure to note any unusual discharge appearing at the vulva of the female. Ask a veterinarian or scientist knowledgeable in laboratory animal reproduction to review your husbandry methods and the genetic background of your breeding stock.

Identification and Record Keeping

When you raise rats, identification and record keeping are important aspects of a suc-

cessful breeding program. Often, the size and similarity between animals makes identification challenging. You will want to keep accurate records of which breeding pairs produce the healthiest offspring, with the best temperaments and most attractive coats and colors.

Cage cards are attached to the cages and are used to record the name or identification number of each animal, its sex, date of birth, and identifying marks or colors. In addition to the group cage card, a separate card or notebook page can be maintained for each individual animal. Individual animal records include weights, breeding dates, date of parturition, number of pups in a litter, the number of live pups at weaning, notes on temperament, and any other valuable pieces of information.

Marking pens: Rats can be marked on their tails with nontoxic marking pens. The identification marks will usually last two to three weeks. Animals will need to be remarked regularly.

Hair clipping: Small amounts of hair can be clipped from different areas of the body for temporary identification.

Hair dye: Nontoxic hair dye can be used in small amounts on specific areas of the body for temporary identification.

Microchips are a form of permanent identification, but they require a handheld scanner to read the identification numbers. Although the microchips are reasonably priced, the scanners can be expensive, although they are very useful for breeding facilities that raise large numbers of animals.

Mutations

Mutations in genes can cause an organ or other body part to develop abnormally, and a birth defect sometimes called a "congenital defect" occurs. Sometimes a mutation gives an animal a survival advantage. If this trait is passed on through the offspring, eventually those members of a species that possess that advantage will out-compete and survive over the disadvantaged. (This is the basis for the theory of evolution or the "survival of the fittest.")

Scientists know more about the rat's genes than about the genes of most other warm-blooded animal. From studies, we know that some out-of-the-ordinary occurrences at birth are really not so out-of-the-ordinary at all. Consider that some animals might be born with extra toes. Certainly we have all seen extra-toed cats. This trait is called "polydactyly" and it can occur in any species. Fused toes, extra teats, absence of a tail or ears, sparse haircoat, no whiskers—these are examples of structure variation that probably would be of no consequence to the pet rat except that one might think that a bald rat would get chilly in the winter!

Some birth defects in rats are the result of outside influences, like drugs or chemicals, rather than genetic mutations. A pup may be born highly underdeveloped or malformed. Some genetic defects might cause a physical difference that is not noticeable at birth, but rather as the rat grows and can be compared with normally developing siblings. Spastic movements, circling, shaking, cataracts, and blindness may appear around the time of weaning. More than one problem can occur in a single animal.

Some of these genetic defects are very well studied by scientists and geneticists. Strains of rats carrying these genes have been nurtured, because the diseases mimic similar disease and disorders in people. Scientists study the gene's effects in the hope of finding a way to eliminate them.

If you have to judge the quality of life of one of your young rats, consider carefully. If the rat is listless, uninterested in food or interaction, and is easily harmed or injured, your veterinarian can end its life humanely. But if the rat eats, enjoys the companionship of its own kind, can move about without injury, and is curious and inquisitive about its surroundings, then the choice for life is probably a good one.

INFORMATION

Clubs and Organizations

For information on breeders and rescue groups in your area, articles and forums on rat care and breeding, meetings, shows and other local events, links to other national and international clubs and personal web pages, check out these clubs and their web pages.

Rat and Mouse Club of America
www.rmca.org
publication: *Rat and Mouse Gazette*

Rodent Fancy
www.RodentFancy.com
publication: *Rat and Mouse Fancy Report*

National Fancy Rat Society (U.K.)
www.nfrs.org
publication: *Pro-Rat-A*

The London and Southern Counties Mouse and Rat Club (U.K.)
www.miceandrats.com

Australian Rat Fanciers Society (Australia)
www.ausrfs.org.au

Animal Rescue Web Sites

www.aspca.org
www.petfinder.org
www.petshelter.org

Personal Web Sites

There are many personal web sites on the Internet devoted to rats as pets. These are particularly well known among rat fanciers, and are useful, if not entertaining, and enrich the human-rat bond.

www.wererat.net
The Wererat's Lair. Totally cool.

RatFanClub.org
This is the personal web site for "The Rat Lady," Debbie Ducommun, widely recognized around the world as one of the most knowledgeable and experienced people on rat care.

Additional Reading

Bucsis, Gerry, and Barbara Sommerville. *Training Your Pet Rat.* Barron's Educational Series, Inc., 2000.

Bulla, Gisela. *Fancy Rats, A Complete Pet Owner's Manual.* Barron's Educational Series, Inc., 1999.

Cardinal, Ginger. *The Rat: An Owner's Guide to a Happy, Healthy Pet.* Hungry Minds, Inc., 1997.

Ducommun, Debbie. *Rats! A Fun and Care Book,* Bowtie Press, 1998.

Ducommun, Debbie. *Rat Health Care.* Available through the author at 857 Lindo Lane, Chico, CA 95973. Also available on the web site (see preceding page).

Harkness, John, and Joseph Wagner. *The Biology and Medicine of Rabbits and Rodents,* 5th ed. Wiley-Blackwell, 2010.

Quesenberry, Katherine, and James Carpenter. *Ferrets, Rabbits, and Rodents: Clinical Medicine and Surgery,* 3rd ed. W. B. Saunders Co., 2011.

National Research Council. *Companion Guide to Infectious Diseases of Mice and Rats.* Nabu Press, 2011.

For Children

Cox, Judy. *Third Grade Pet.* Holiday House, 1998.

Erlbach, Arlene. *My Pet Rat.* Lerner Publications, 1998.

Glaser, Linda. *Rosie's Birthday Rat.* Dell Publishing Group, 1996.

Grahame, Kenneth. *Wind in the Willows.* Various publishers.

O'Brien, Robert. *Mrs. Frisby and the Rats of Nimh.* Various publishers.

INDEX

About the Authors

Dr. Carol Himsel Daly lives in Connecticut with her family and practices small animal medicine and surgery. In her spare time she enjoys writing, cooking, gardening, and especially seeing the world through the eyes of a 6-year-old.

Sharon Vanderlip, D.V.M., has provided veterinary care to exotic, wild, and domestic animals for more than 30 years. She has published scientific journals and has authorized more than 20 books on pet care. Dr. Vanderlip owns a specialty practice and previously served as clinical veterinarian for the University of California at San Diego School of Medicine. She has collaborated on research projects with the San Diego Zoo and is former chief of veterinary services for the National Aeronautics and Space Administration. Dr. Vanderlip has cared for and treated countless rats during her professional career. She may be contacted for seminars at *www.sharonvanderlip.com*

Photo Credits

Sharon Vanderlip: pages 4, 14, 31, 32, 39, 80, 81; Jacquelynn Holly: pages 5, 35, 62; Shutterstock: pages 2–3, 7, 9, 10, 12, 13, 15, 16, 18, 21, 22, 23, 24, 25, 26, 27, 28, 29, 30, 33, 34, 36, 37, 38, 40, 42, 43, 44, 45, 46, 47, 48, 49, 50, 51, 53, 54, 55, 57, 59, 60, 63, 64, 65, 66, 71, 72, 75, 76, 78, 82, 83, 84, 85, 86, 87 (top and bottom), 88, 89, 90, 91, 92, 93, 95.

Cover Photos

Shutterstock: front cover, back cover, inside front cover, inside back cover.

Important Note

There are a few diseases of domestic rats that can be transmitted to humans (see page 77). If your rat shows any sign of illness, you should definitely call the veterinarian, and if you are at all worried that your own health might be affected, consult your doctor.

Some people are allergic to animal urine, dander, and saliva. If you think you might have such an allergy, check with your doctor before bringing home a rat.

Dedication

To Snudge and his kind.

Acknowledgments

I would like to thank the many people who gave praise to the first edition of this book, and encouragement and suggestions for this revision. I would especially like to mention Karen Grant, R.N., Cheryl Stewart, Jo Norris, and Donell Meadows for their kind correspondence and contributions.

All inquiries should be addressed to:
Barron's Educational Series, Inc.
250 Wireless Boulevard
Hauppauge, NY 11788
www.barronseduc.com

ISBN: 978-0-7641-4745-6

Library of Congress Control Number: 2012939801

Printed in China
9 8 7 6 5 4 3 2 1